Don't Pray ... Without Passion!

The How To's of Effective Prayer

Marilyn Sampson

Sovereign World

Sovereign World Ltd
PO Box 777
Tonbridge
Kent
TN11 0ZS
England

ISBN 1 85240 230 X

The publishers aim to produce books which will help to extend and build up the Kingdom of God. We do not necessarily agree with every view expressed by the author, or with every interpretation of Scripture expressed. We expect each reader to make his/her judgement in the light of their own understanding of God's Word and in an attitude of Christian love and fellowship.

Typeset by CRB Associates, Reepham, Norfolk.
Printed in the United States of America.

Acknowledgements

My heartfelt thanks to our dear friends, Fred and Betty Hicks, for their hard work and sacrifice of time on this manuscript. Thank you for being willing instruments of the Lord. May He reward you in an awesome way!

Sincere appreciation and gratitude to my husband, Steve, who has labored with me on this endeavor.

Thanks too to our precious daughter, Brittani, for being so patient with her mother over these past months. I greatly appreciate all your help, support, encouragement, enthusiasm and creative ideas for this book. Thank you to our son, David, for assisting with all the intricate computer 'stuff' on this book and for your prayer support. And many thanks to our beautiful daughter, Kristi, for all the prayers she directed my way. Sixteen years ago she decorated and crafted by hand the first prayer journal I ever owned, which marked the beginning of my recording the glorious and life-changing truths the Lord has spoken into me over that period of time.

Contents

Author's Note

Throughout this book I have included, along with the teaching, many literal statements that the Holy Spirit has spoken to me over many years. Most of these I have gleaned from sixteen years of journal entries.

He spoke the majority of these statements to me (which cover a diversity of subjects) as I was praying. Therefore, since there are a number of these statements throughout the book, I have chosen to simply put each of them in quotes and bold type. Other words or statements in bold type, but without quotes, are merely for emphasis.

As you read this book, it will be obvious when you observe these bold quotes, that these are the precise words the Holy Spirit spoke to me regarding the subject at hand.

Marilyn Sampson
January 2001

Introduction

There is no greater satisfaction in life than the spirit within us, which has been created by God, communing with its Creator. **'Nothing in life compares to deep calling to deep'** (see Psalm 42:7).

Prayer is the **only** way to stay in touch with what is transpiring in the Kingdom of God. It is through prayer that we remain in sync with the heart-beat of God. Prayer is not a thing, but a spiritual flow. It is not cerebral, it is birthed. It is a constant creative process orchestrated by the Holy Spirit as He 'births' things forth.

Prayer should never be general, but rather specific and strategic, as the mind of the Father is being continuously revealed. **'Vague prayers do not intimidate the devil.'** People must **know** the mind of God. Formulas, clichés, and parroted sermons will not make an impact for the Kingdom of God.

Prayer always has a strategy and a divine purpose. Habitually, we must be sensitive to the thoughts and strategies of God, so that precious time is never wasted praying repetitious generalities, but all our energy is expended toward divinely directed Holy Spirit targets.

What is received fresh from the throne through the vehicle of prayer and listening will bring life and results.

In this book I offer my own personal experiences explaining the truths the Holy Spirit taught me regarding praying with strategies and listening for His explicit directives.

Chapter 1

God's Agenda or Man's?

'When you yield to your own agenda
you cease being creative.'

*'Most assuredly, I say to you, the Son can do **nothing** of
Himself, but what He sees the Father do; for whatever He
does, the Son also does in like manner.'*
(John 5:19)

'Pray longer' were the strong words of admonition I heard
from the Lord as I headed for the exit ramp of the interstate,
on my daily early-morning 'prayer driving vigil' in my prayer
closet on wheels.

The Lord did not enlighten me for whom, or why, I was to
continue praying that day, but I **knew** in my spirit something serious was being diverted through the vehicle of
prayer. I also had confidence that, for whomever intercession
was being directed, many other obedient 'listeners' would
also heed the Father's directive to pray and intercede.

There is a great necessity to respond immediately and to
yield when God speaks to us. It can literally make a life or
death difference.

Later that same day, the urgency of the Lord's previous
admonition for extended intercession became crystal clear,
when I learned my husband was involved in a near-tragic car
accident. After taking medication (to which he was unknow-
ingly severely allergic) to alleviate pain from a root canal, he
lost consciousness while driving down a major highway in

our city. Before he 'came to' his vehicle crossed two lanes of speeding traffic, continued inexorably onward over the center median, crossed two more lanes of traffic – all before careening off a steep embankment, hitting several trees on the way down, and stopping just short of a river.

People in nearby vehicles watched in helpless disbelief and horror as the scenario unfolded as if in slow motion before their eyes. Most concluded that my husband had suffered a heart attack while behind the wheel.

911 was immediately called, but by the time help arrived, my husband had regained consciousness and assured all the disbelieving bystanders that he would indeed be fine ... eventually – realizing he had experienced a severe reaction to the pain medication.

Praying as you hear God's thoughts

Hearing from God and praying are synonymous. The devil comes to steal, kill and destroy (John 10:10), and roams about as a roaring lion seeking whom he may devour (1 Peter 5:6–8), but we are able, through 'strategic prayer', to literally head-off potential tragedies and disasters at the pass.

'*No weapon formed against you shall prosper*' (Isaiah 54:17) is a popular Scripture we all like to quote, but without the sensitivity to **hear God's voice** (on which I will specifically elaborate in Chapter 6) and skillfully utilize our 'spiritual weapons' of prayer and the exercise of spiritual authority, it is difficult to disengage the plans and devices of the devil being schemed against us.

We are never to fear the enemy, but we must recognize that he is a shrewd strategist (roaming about), scheming constantly against unprotected or vulnerable prey. **We must** out-strategize him. We should always remain alert and on the offensive, never allowing him to put us on the defensive.

> '*Be of sober spirit, **be on the alert**. Your adversary, the devil, prowls about like a roaring lion, seeking **someone** to devour.*'
> (1 Peter 5:8 NASB)

God's initiative or ours?

As we learn to flow with the Spirit, and discern God's **initiative** – we become increasingly aware of His desires and intentions – and **'all our prayers can be effectual and pack a powerful punch.'** There is no question that through prayer, destinies are fulfilled; lives are transformed; disasters are averted and the Kingdom of God is manifest on the earth.

The only way to have God's initiative is to stay in His 'solar system' – that awesome dimension of the Spirit realm . To see and hear what the Father is doing, we must stay on supernatural 'airways' by continually yielding our carnal minds to His higher purposes. He reveals to our hearts what we should pray about, then as we do His purpose is 'birthed' in the Spirit through the vehicle of prayer.

Undeniably, prayer is the most misunderstood tool and opportunity that God has made available to the believer. It is the greatest power in the universe to which Christians have access, and is probably the most under-utilized gift God has given to man. Prayer was never meant to be a chore or obligation, but rather a **privilege** and a **joy**.

Walking with God is a bit like having Christmas everyday. We don't **have** to pray and commune with Him, but we **get** to.

The believer's intimacy and communication with God are the key to fruitfulness, joy and contentment beyond words. A life of fellowship with the Holy Spirit is the **greatest venture** a person can ever experience.

We must know Him and desire His mind

Jesus' highest priority was to **know** the mind of the Father. Clearly then, this should also be the paramount motive in our lives. He was totally dependent on His communication with His Father as He attempted **nothing** on His **own** initiative (see John 5:19).

Jesus is our greatest example. As we purpose to pray as He did, we will begin to **know** God's thoughts and to pray with powerful effectiveness.

Our goal in life should be to do nothing except what we see and hear the Father doing. God can only be creative and supernatural, which means we must ascend to His realm and exchange our thoughts and ways for His.

> '"For My thoughts are not your thoughts, nor are your ways My ways," says the LORD. "For as the heavens are higher than the earth, so are My ways **higher** than your ways, and My thoughts than your thoughts."'
>
> (Isaiah 55:8–9)

Obviously our thoughts are not God's, but His thoughts **are attainable** if we ask for them. God wants to be in **all** our thoughts so we become 'God-conscious' instead of 'self-conscious'.

Have a funeral for your self-will daily

Jesus did nothing except that which He **saw** by the Spirit. We don't have the luxury of yielding to our own agenda or opinions (Jesus lived a perpetual fast from His own thoughts and opinions). We must only listen for His creative Word and obey.

We need to have a funeral for our self-will every day before breakfast so we can rise above every distraction and carnal thought and focus on becoming God-conscious. Then His thoughts will be in **all** we do and our day can be orchestrated by Him. The carnal mind is hostility (hatred) against God (Romans 8:7). We must constantly be renewed in our minds (Romans 12:1–2) – an indication that a transformation is continually taking place in which we exchange our thoughts for His divine thoughts.

Prayer is the **key** that takes us out of the flesh and into the Spirit. We are captive to our own flesh until we yield to His thoughts.

As we press in to God through prayer and call forth that which we see and hear by the Spirit, every prayer we pray will command an answer.

Assurance of answered prayer

Clearly, if we are **not** open to God's agenda and His thoughts, we cut off the creative flow He willingly desires to make available to us.

When we enter into prayer desiring to seek the Lord, it is amazing how we find ourselves praying for things different from that which we had planned. That is, because when we enter into the presence of the Lord, He begins to reveal His agenda; He directs us to pray the **heart** of the Father. When we pray His will and mind we are **assured** the prayer is being answered. I used to begin prayer with a list of needs or requests, but as I matured I knew I had to put the list away and pray what was **fresh** on His heart at that moment.

Unselfish motives

There is nothing more pleasing to God than when we pray with **unselfish motives**. Jesus told us to pray 'Thy Kingdom come' not '**my** kingdom come.' If we practice praying the needs of the Kingdom, our prayer life, as well as our natural life, will change. If we pray selfishly, our prayer life simply takes on our own carnal nature. No prayers are answered more quickly than those we pray unselfishly with the motive to see the Kingdom of God increased.

> *'But seek **first** the Kingdom of God and His righteousness, and all these **things** shall be **added to you**.'*
>
> (Matthew 6:33)

Bob Cornwall, an evangelist and Bible teacher, had a vision years ago that he was in heaven. There was a huge conveyor belt going down to the earth with many packages on it. In the vision, Jesus was crying as the packages (the answers to prayers) were filled with mundane, material things such as clothing and other items people on earth had prayed for. God was faithful to answer their prayers, although they came from selfish motives. Then suddenly, there came a loud marimba sound from the earth. The prayers had changed.

People's hearts had turned and they were asking for the increase of the Kingdom of God. Then a large brown package (with answers to Kingdom prayers) was being sent on the conveyor belt to earth. However the outside of it was covered with sparkles and illuminates (representing 'things' being added along with the answer to the Kingdom prayers). This time Jesus was smiling, because people were no longer praying selfishly but seeking first the Kingdom, and all the 'other things' were added to them as well.

Instead of praying Kingdom strategies, our time in prayer is often spent in expressing all **our** problems and needs to God. Yet the Scriptures clearly state if we seek **first** the Kingdom (**asking God what the needs of the Kingdom are**) then 'all these things shall be added unto us.' Naturally, He will take care of our 'stuff' if we are mindful of the Kingdom and yield to His agenda and initiatives. Asking God for our personal needs is the least important of all prayers, yet this accounts for the majority of all prayers prayed. Instead of praying about all our worldly needs and worries, we just need to focus on 'touching' Him.

If we yield ourselves to God's business, He'll move for us. If we ignore the needs of the Kingdom and center on self, we'll receive minuscule results.

What is the Kingdom really?

Just as asking people how their family is doing blesses them, equally it is a blessing to the Lord if we inquire about the needs of **His** family and **His** Kingdom. Therefore, it is wisdom to ask the Lord how we can pray specifically to increase His Kingdom, and not simply ask Him to meet our own needs.

I remember one time when my daughter was around ten years old. She approached me in the kitchen asking if there was anything she could do to help. After I regained consciousness, I stated, 'As a matter of fact there are some things you could help me with.' As we mature, we should enter into the presence of the Lord and first ask what are the needs of His Kingdom. Maybe we will hear a loud crash, as He faints from shock!

A good way to define maturity is simply not thinking of 'self' and 'our needs' first. Secondly, it is seeing a need and meeting it without being told. Children do things when they are **told** to do them, but a mature person does them without being told.

When our prayer lives change, everything else changes with them. Prayer is an investment in the Kingdom of God. It is an investment of time and a discipline unto God. Through prayer, lives are changed; circumstances are altered; and priorities come into focus. **'You are laying up treasures no man can touch.'**

While meditating on the Lord's prayer (Matthew 6), I asked the Lord, 'What is the Kingdom?' He spoke to me the following words:

- **'It is the Father's business.'** Jesus was building the Kingdom as He was about His Father's business (Luke 2:49). We too must have pure motives to see the Kingdom of God increased.

- **'It is your sphere of responsibility.'** (Your family and those whom God has placed around you.)

  'We, however, will not boast beyond measure, but within the limits of the sphere which God appointed us – a sphere which especially includes you.'   (2 Corinthians 10:13)

  This means calling forth the destiny, hunger, giftings and so on, in each person within our sphere, as directed by the Spirit. It is wise when praying for someone close to you, to pray unselfishly – in other words, leave yourself out of the prayer. Many pray for the Lord to change others, simply to make their own lives smoother. But the prayer that is answered quickly is the one that asks the Lord to bring about change for that person's sake, for Jesus' sake, and for the sake of the Kingdom of God.

- **'It is your brother's weakness.'** (The needs of the body of Christ.) Let God give the specifics of whom to pray for and how to pray.

- **'It is hearing with conciseness.'** God will be specific and direct. He may not speak a paragraph, but He will tell you exactly what to pray. One word or sentence from God changes everything.

• **'It is praying, "Not my will, but Thine."'** (His Kingdom comes first.) Our motive must be for the will of God. Very often while in prayer, I hear these words rise out of my spirit, 'Come forth, Kingdom.' I have learned that as I yield solely to **His agenda**, putting my own requests aside, He will powerfully direct my prayers and Kingdom business will get done. Frequently, I will hear the name of a certain nation about which I may not be terribly knowledgeable. No matter, as I follow the flow of this, I know His will is being accomplished in that land. He has promised, as part of our inheritance, to give us the nations (Psalm 2). Also, I frequently receive directives on specifically how to pray for our nation; our city; those in places of leadership, and specific people with specific needs. The point is, if we are endeavoring to seek first His Kingdom and His righteousness, then there will not only be assured results, but God has clearly promised that all these things (our personal needs included) shall be 'added unto us' and those in our families (see Matthew 6:33).

We must strive to be **imitators** of God – those who do what God does, who say what God says. Faith is not a technique that we hope to develop. It is an attitude of the **heart** that comes when we learn that we can do **nothing** of ourselves.

*'Therefore be **imitators** of God as dear children. And walk in love, as Christ also has loved us and **given Himself** for us, an offering and a sacrifice to God for a sweet-smelling aroma.'*   (Ephesians 5:1–2)

Prayer and hearing the voice of God should go hand in hand. Thank God for the Holy Spirit who promises to guide us and lead us. Anytime we pray we should expect and anticipate that the Spirit of God will speak to us specifically, telling us what to pray and how to pray. It is much more exciting to hear what God wants us to pray, than to pray our own agenda.

Chapter 2

Get Ready for Increase!

'Spiritual abortion will occur if you do not
aggressively birth forth God's destiny in your life.'

'Where there is no vision, the people perish.'
(Proverbs 29:18 KJV)

God desires to bring **increase** in every area of our lives.
Naturally, He wants us to grow spiritually – *'... to be strengthened with might through His Spirit in the inner man'* (Ephesians
3:16), but He also desires for us to **increase** in fruitfulness and
to **expand** into the destiny He has purposed for us.

1 Chronicles chapter 4 lists the details of the 'family tree'
of the tribe of Judah. One particular descendant, Jabez
(whose name meant 'one who causes pain'), is recorded as
crying out to the Lord,

> *'Oh, that You would bless me indeed, and **enlarge** my
> territory* [borders].' (1 Chronicles 4:10)

Jabez received his name because his mother experienced so
much pain giving birth to him. His destiny was to 'cause
pain', but wishing to break out of this 'life sentence', He cried
out to God. He prayed an unselfish prayer, a prayer for
increase and enlarged borders that would take him beyond
his earthly destiny into the fullness of God's blessing. We
should always pray for increase – for more of God, more
anointing, more understanding, and greater fruitfulness.

> *'Of the increase of His government and peace there will be no end.'*
> (Isaiah 9:7)

Calling things forth

The power of prayer is so awesome that **we** can **call forth** our destiny. In prayer, we can call forth with clarity the specific vision God has for our lives.

> *'Where there is no vision, the people perish.'*
> (Proverbs 29:18 KJV)

We can call forth increased fruitfulness, opportunities and outlets and, most of all, **souls** for the increase of the Kingdom. For our children and spouse, we can daily call forth (along with other specifics the Lord may speak to us) their godly destiny in life, His giftings within them, and for constant spiritual hunger. Ministers can call forth doors of fruitfulness; businessmen can call forth doors of opportunity; Christians can call forth God's favor in their lives. The list is endless. We need to come boldly into His Throne Room daily, asking for enlargement and increase in every area of our lives, so that His plans and purposes for us will be fulfilled in this earth (each day).

We hold the key to the creative

When the Holy Spirit speaks, His words always contain creative power, but we have to become willing instruments to call forth His will and purpose and then embrace what He declares.

Romans 4:17 tells us that God is the One who, *'...gives life to the dead and calls those things which do not exist as though they did.'* God declares that something is so, before it physically exists. In His view there is no difference between the things that actually exist now, and the things that He is calling into existence.

The key for us as God's children is that we too, must first 'see' with our spiritual eyes the things that the Father is calling us to pray about, then call them forth through prayer and declaration. We will then witness the incredible miracle of prayer as we see the intangible become tangible. Anyone can believe what the **natural eyes** see, but it takes **knowing the mind of the Spirit** to call forth that which is not obvious.

Perhaps the greatest lack in praying believers is the understanding that **they** can call forth 'open doors' and opportunities through prayer. Persistent, consistent prayer can be likened to the passionate request of a child who has a special desire, and continually 'reminds' the parent, who has the ability and resources to make it come to pass. Equally, God can be entreated to bring forth greater opportunities and results in our lives. An example is the persistent widow who approached the unrighteous judge, who had neither fear of God nor man. This widow continually approached the judge with the **same** request, **until** he provided her the legal protection she was asking for. The judge (whom Jesus likened Himself to in the parable) answered the widow only because of her persistent desire.

> *'Yet because this widow continues to bother me, I will defend and protect and avenge her; lest she give me intolerable annoyance and **wear me out by her continual coming, or at the last she come and rail on me, or assault me, or strangle me.'*** (Luke 18:5 Amp)

Our potential destiny may sit dormant until we 'press in' to God by calling forth these greater opportunities in our lives.

Every believer can call forth souls. As we ask God for souls (and opportunities and strategies to win them) God will answer.

> *'**Ask** of me, and I shall give thee the heathen for **thine inheritance**, and the uttermost parts of the earth for thy possession.'* (Psalm 2:8 KJV)

God plainly tells **us** that we should,

> '...**ask**, *and it will be given to you;* **seek**, *and you will find;* **knock**, *and it will be opened to you. For everyone who asks receives, and he who seeks finds, and to him who knocks it will be opened.'*   (Luke 11:9–10)

God is waiting for us to call it forth!

I earnestly sought the Lord about what causes our spirits (our inner man) to grow. He revealed to me three specific areas.

1. **Consecrated prayer (Builds).** True prayer builds up the inner man just as intense exercise builds up the outer man (the muscles of our physical body). Once you begin to consecrate yourself to committed and regular prayer, hearing the voice of the Lord speak to you and through you is inevitable. Spiritual growth is certain when a believer begins to communicate with the Holy Spirit.

2. **The light of revelation (Feeds).** Paul prayed for the church at Ephesus, '...*that the God of our Lord Jesus Christ, the Father of glory, may give to you the spirit of wisdom and revelation in the knowledge of Him'* (Ephesians 1:17), '...*by having the eyes of your heart flooded with light'* (Ephesians 1:18 Amp). Revelation from the Holy Spirit **feeds** your spirit. God brings 'light' into our understanding to make 'hidden things' understood.

3. **Giving out (Exercise).** There is nothing that causes our spirits to grow more quickly than when we 'give out' what God has given us. Whether it is yielding to the gifts of the Spirit, giving encouragement, or pouring ourselves into others lives, growth is certain. **'No one can become strong by watching someone else exercise.'**

Avoid spiritual abortions

Anytime God talks, His words contain creative power. Just like Mary **we have to say**, *'Let it be to me according to Your word'* (Luke 1:38).

It is important to receive and embrace anything that God says to us. Believers often commit 'spiritual abortion' because they do not embrace the words the Holy Spirit speaks to them. God's words to us must be **received** so there will be a 'birthing' and a bringing forth of what He speaks to us.

When we don't pray we also commit spiritual abortion. If Hannah had not cried out to God (1 Samuel chapter 1) there would have been no Samuel (or her five other children) to fulfill God's destiny. Prayer is where **conception** takes place. There must be a birthing process (intercession) taking place with the believer or there will be no manifestation of God's purposes. We will fall short of our full potential and God's destiny for us, if the birth process isn't working in us.

Because the natural mind rejects and dismisses what it doesn't understand, anyone can be guilty of committing spiritual abortion. We must live with a willingness to embrace the mind of the Spirit at all times.

Increase in the gifts of the Spirit

One extremely significant area to pray for is an increase in the gifts of the Spirit operating through us. Paul said, *'Pursue love and **desire** spiritual gifts, but **especially** that you may prophesy'* (1 Corinthians 14:1). Prophecy is so important because people need encouraging, plus the prophetic word calls forth the potential in people's lives.

Recently, we were ministering in a church in northern Alabama. I was so moved by the Lord during a time of ministry to speak to a young married couple. I was amazed as the word of the Lord came through me saying to them, 'God says you are sold out to Him.' The Holy Spirit kept emphasizing through the prophecy that this young couple were indeed sold out to God. Suddenly the young man stood up and asked if he could say something. He told the crowd, 'This lady doesn't know me and she has no way of knowing that my wife and I are youth pastors; and the name of our youth group is "Sold Out!"' Needless to say, the prophetic word of the Lord greatly encouraged them.

The following evening, the Lord impressed on me to pray for a man in the crowd of several hundred people. As I prayed for him, the Holy Spirit showed me a picture of him throwing out a life-line (as to a drowning person). The pastor told my husband and me later that this man has a large cassette tape ministry, sending out two thousand tapes a month, and the name he operates under is 'Life-line Ministries.' What a great comfort this confirming word was to this man.

God is willing to give each of us more in the realm of the Spirit. All we have to do is ask!

> *'Do not despise prophecies.'*   (1 Thessalonians 5:20)

Is resistance our friend?

Another thing that causes spiritual growth is resistance. When resistance from the enemy occurs in our lives, God uses it so we will exercise our spiritual muscles. If you encounter resistance, rejoice! You are worth being resisted.

Resistance and trials mean one thing – that **promotion and increase are coming**! That is why James proclaimed, *'...count* [calculate] *it all joy when you fall into various trials'* (James 1:2).

Just as in school, when there are exams (which most dread), increase follows. Promotion to the next level is inevitable. Equally, following trials, God takes us to a new level!

You can't be 'tried' without God putting something in you that wasn't there before. Pray and believe that your prayer life and what others see in you, might have a **greater influence** as a result. Peter went through numerous trials, but God brought his life to the place where even **his shadow brought results**.

> *'...so that they brought the sick out into the streets and laid them on beds and couches, that at least **the shadow of Peter** passing by might fall on some of them.'*   (Acts 5:15)

God desires to bring us to the place where the very 'shadow' of our lives influence people for the Kingdom of

God. It is what He has **done** in our lives that causes effectiveness – not just what we say or know through gathered knowledge. Peter said to the crippled man, *'But what I do have I give you'* (Acts 3:6).

He is glorified when our lives touch and influence others. Through prayer, we can see His hand bring forth increase not only to our lives, but for countless people.

Yielded vessels

It is a known fact that Smith Wigglesworth, a great British evangelist who lived and ministered in the early 1900s, was so completely sold out to God that frequently unsaved people who happened to be near him would fall under tremendous conviction by the Holy Spirit. Someone could be seated next to him on a park bench or on a train, and without him even engaging them in conversation, the presence of the Lord emanating through Wigglesworth was so strong that the person would begin to weep and be overwhelmed with conviction about the lost state of his soul. Naturally, Wigglesworth used every opportunity to lead such people to Christ.

I have known in my lifetime men and women of God that were so dead to self and so full of God that people in all stations in life would be drawn to their presence, not really knowing why. I have witnessed waitresses, store clerks, airline stewardesses, and people in public places 'fall' under the convicting influence of these godly men and women, and many lives have been transformed as a result.

I know every believer can reach that place of **influence** in his life, if he is willing to pay the price. We can live in a realm in God where we are so dead to self and the pull of the world, and so yielded to the Holy Spirit, that merely our presence can cause people to take notice and be eternally affected.

The people of this world's system are full of darkness, unrest, anxieties and worries, consumed with self and void of joy. But as we walk in victory and get our minds off self and on God, exuding godly peace and joy, we will undoubtedly influence many to move out of the kingdom of darkness and into God's light. People everywhere are desperately searching for true victory and contentment. We are God's conduit for Him to flow through and affect change in people's lives.

> *'You are the light of the world. A city that is set on a hill cannot be hidden. Nor do they light a lamp and put it under a basket, but on a lampstand, and it gives light to all who are in the house. Let your light so shine before men, that they may see your good works and glorify your Father in heaven.'*
> (Matthew 5:13–15)

Divine stretching or satanic attack?

David knew affliction was not his enemy, but His friend. *'Before I was **afflicted** I went astray,'* he says, *'but now I keep your word'* (Psalm 119:67). He repeats this thought in this Psalm, saying:

> *'It is good for me that I've been **afflicted**, that I may learn your statutes.'*   (Psalm 119:71)

And,

> *'I know, O Lord, that your judgments are right, and that in faithfulness you have **afflicted** me.'*   (Psalm 119:75)

Some believe and teach that **any** trial or affliction that comes your way is directly from Satan and should be rebuked. But even an unsaved person has enough insight to know that the more a person has suffered, the more character building has been accomplished in that one – and that more life and compassion emanates from that person as a result.

Don't rebuke the devil when God is allowing resistance for your own good and strengthening. We must **know** the difference between satanic attack and godly stretching.

God's goal was to strengthen Peter when Jesus said to him,

> *'Simon, Simon! Indeed, Satan has asked for you that he may sift you as wheat. But I have prayed for you, that your*

faith should not fail; and when you have returned to Me,
strengthen your brethren.*'*   (Luke 22:31–32)

Some life-altering statements the Lord has spoken to me
through the years regarding trials and resistance are:

- 'I'm not interested in the comfort of your flesh, but
  the condition of your spirit.'
- 'The more you go back to the potter's wheel, the more
  you will look like Me' (see Jeremiah 18).
- 'Your hardest moments will produce the greatest
  abundance of fruit.'
- 'To develop impeccable character, you must be tried
  and true and tested by fire.'
- 'Obstacles are stepping stones (character builders)
  which make room for more of Me.'
- 'You're no use to the Kingdom of God until you suffer
  and get delivered of self.'

  *'Although He was a son, He learned obedience through the
  things He suffered.'*   (Hebrews 5:8)

- 'If you don't suffer weakness and affliction, you'll
  never know the full strength of the Lord.'
- 'Adversity leads to the cross: it's your friend if you
  befriend it.'

Are trials and suffering really necessary?

We'll never be able to lead others into victory if we can't walk
in it ourselves. Every area of victory that results from trials
we've personally endured, can be applied to the lives of
others. There is no 'hard place' that a believer walks through
(if yielded to God) that will be in vain. The Lord will always
place **new deposits** in us through struggles that will bring
God's life and encouragement to others.

Paul wrote two-thirds of the New Testament in a dark,
dank, dingy jail cell. Yet, look at the wealth beyond measure
that came out of that horrific circumstance.

There were twenty-one attempts in nine years on King David's life. David was anointed by Samuel nine years before being appointed King. Because David was **a man after God's own heart**, he esteemed the anointing and the call of God on Saul, even though Saul's motive was to kill him (see 1 Samuel 24 & 26). However, David was not 'promoted' until he **passed** all the character tests.

Joseph had a grandiose dream of his brothers bowing down to him which, though it spoke about God's ultimate destiny for his life, would lead him on a path through much suffering and hardship before it was fulfilled. Genesis 37:5 says,

> '...Joseph had a dream, and he told it to his brothers; and they hated him even more.'

He suffered unmercifully in prison for twelve years before witnessing a smidgen of breakthrough. Finally, he was promoted to a position second only to Pharaoh, and God had done such a work in him that, when he finally faced his brothers who had betrayed him, he said,

> '"But as for you, you meant evil against me; **but God meant it for good**, in order to bring it about as it is this day, to save many people alive. Now therefore, do not be afraid; I will provide for you and your little ones." And he comforted them and spoke kindly to them.'   (Genesis 50:20–21)

I say all of this, not to imply that God is out to **get** us, but that God is out to **make** us into His image. The more trips we make to the potter's wheel, the more we'll look like Christ, and His characteristics and nature will be more evident in our lives. The more we yield and obey to the workings of the Spirit in and through us, the more spiritual fruit will be accrued in our heavenly bank account. Increase is on the way!

Joy is not debatable

1 Samuel chapter 30 recounts the occasion when King David and his men arrived at Ziklag to find that the Amalekites had

invaded it, burned the city with fire and taken captive all the women and children. It was sink or swim for David. Either he could capitulate to the hateful accusations and death threats of the people, or he could **encourage Himself** in the Lord (1 Samuel 30:6). When he decided to go to the Lord, the Lord spoke to him, saying,

> *'Pursue, for you shall surely overtake them and without fail recover **all**.'* (1 Samuel 30:8)

When you are going through severe trials and testing you have a choice. Either you can remain in a place of weeping, or choose to get out of self-pity and bitterness. I heard someone say, 'Self-pity is Satan's baby sitter without charge.' Your victory quotient is based on how good you are at encouraging yourself.

Bitterness is matured anger, so it must be treated like your worst enemy. It keeps alive the most vile element of the worst things in your life. Bitterness has been likened to a person drinking poison, hoping the other person will die. **'Don't hold grudges as they are crippling.'**

The writer of the book of Hebrews tells us that we should check on ourselves regularly, examining our heart and attitudes and,

> *'Looking carefully lest anyone fall short of the grace of God; lest any **root of bitterness** springing up cause trouble, and by this ... become defiled.'* (Hebrews 12:15)

Realize that when torment and discouragement come against you, its because the devil is losing ground. You are **worth** being resisted!

Joy produces **patience** (a cheerful consistency) which produces **testimony** (evidence of God working in our lives) that we may become perfect, in need of nothing. James said,

> *' ... let patience have its perfect work, that you may be perfect and complete, lacking nothing.'* (James 1:4)

Your best and your worst days can produce joy. Hardship produces a testimony over time. Encourage yourself in God to rise above hard times. Trials should go into the 'joy column' of our portfolio of Christian experiences.

Keep your eyes on the finish line!

> *'Therefore we also, since we are surrounded by so great a cloud of witnesses, let us lay aside **every weight**, and the sin which so easily ensnares us, and let us run with endurance the race that is set before us, looking unto Jesus, the author and finisher of our faith, who for the **joy** that was set before Him **endured the cross**, despising the shame, and has sat down at the right hand of the throne of God.'*   (Hebrews 12:1–2)

We must focus on the finish line and lay aside every weight or hindrance. No one can run effectively with weights on. We must look beyond the immediate circumstances and 'see' the victory.

Looking at circumstances is serpents' food. We must shake the dust (serpents' food) off our feet and anticipate what God has in store. We can't see what the Father is seeing if we are looking down. Speak to the contrary circumstances through the power of prayer.

> *'Death and life are in the power of the tongue, and those who love it will eat its fruit.'*   (Proverbs 18:21)

We have the authority to command **every** mountain to move.

Don't be weak, but bold in your requests!

Come boldly into the Throne Room. **'Be bold in your requests!'**

> *'Let us therefore come boldly to the throne of grace, that we may obtain mercy and find grace to help in time of need.'*
>   (Hebrews 4:16)

Access the Father and **ask**, believing **beyond** what you presently have, both spiritually and naturally. Ask for souls, a greater anointing, major doors of opportunity, greater results and breakthroughs. **'Don't be puny in your belief.'** Focus on the Spirit, not the natural (obtain God's perspective on situations and abolish the world's way of thinking).

We tend to pray about things in man's terms and dimensions. Instead we should pray for Kingdom strategies to come. Pray for doors of influence and pray for other lands (opportunities) to open.

Passion is the birthplace of dreams. Passion is the difference between those who get things done and those who don't.

Increase!

The Lord intends to bring us increase upon increase.

David said, *'You have set my feet in a **wide** place'* (Psalm 31:8), and *'You **enlarged** my path under me, so my feet did not slip'* (Psalm 18:36). He doesn't want us to remain at the same level; He desires that we should go from **glory to glory** (2 Corinthians 3:18). If He brought increase to Peter, so that even his shadow was causing people to be healed, how much more does He want to do through us, as we let Him bring forth His nature in us? The possibilities are endless. Let's set our vision high, as God has 'big things' in store for all of us. In the early church there was continual increase and, *'...the word of God grew and multiplied'* (Acts 12:24).

> *'**Enlarge** the place of your tent, and let them stretch out the curtains of your dwellings; **do not spare**; lengthen your cords, and strengthen your stakes. For **you** shall expand to the right and to the left...'*   (Isaiah 54:2–3)

Chapter 3

Praying Passionately with Strategies

'Strategies are like avenues, they get you where you want to go.'

'Strategic prayer obscures the enemy's blueprints.'

'Therefore I run thus: not with uncertainty. Thus I fight: not as one who beats the air.'
(1 Corinthians 9:26)

The ultimate strategist

'**God is the ultimate strategist who possesses unlimited power. The devil** (on the other hand) **is a powerful strategist who possesses limited power.**'

God's Word tells us that the 'weapons of our warfare' against the devil are 'mighty for the pulling down of strongholds' – but they remain useless if we don't know how to utilize them. God's people must be skilled in 'divine weaponry' and ever sensitive to hearing God's voice and His divine directives.

Our weapons (which are prayer and spiritual authority) are divinely powerful, but the devil will take advantage of our ignorance if we do not seek God for specific strategies to engage them. The devil schemes, reasons, plans and implements strategies against us. He will only flee when we resist Him (James 4:17). His strategy is to keep us always on the defensive, patching leaks and plugging holes. His schemes never cease, but we can **diffuse** them. Strategic prayer will quash the enemy's plans.

Strongholds have to bow

The Bible also tells us that 'No weapon formed against us can prosper' (see Isaiah 54:17), but again we must seek God's direction in order to **know** by the Spirit which specific weapons and strategies are being fashioned against us. What area of vulnerability in us is the devil seeking to attack? Armed with this knowledge we are able to 'head him off at the pass' before anything can take root. But we must first have knowledge from God on the devices the devil has commissioned against us at his most recent committee meeting in hell.

The Bible also assures us that, as children of God, we are more than conquerors in every situation. Greater is He that is in us than he that is in the world (1 John 4:4). However, we are defenseless and become easy prey for the enemy without our armor and God-given strategies. Our armor won't help us if we don't know how to use it.

Paul says in his letter to the Ephesians,

> 'Put on the **whole armor** of God, that you may be able to stand against the wiles of the devil ... Stand therefore, having **girded your waist with truth**, having put on the **breastplate of righteousness**, and having **shod your feet** with the preparation of the gospel of peace; above all, taking the **shield of faith** with which you will be able to quench all the fiery darts of the wicked one. And take the **helmet of salvation**, and the **sword of the Spirit**, which is the word of God; **praying always with all prayer and supplication in the Spirit** ... '   (Ephesians 6:11–18)

Notice that praying in the Spirit is part of the armor! We need to know what works to keep us in a victorious posture. We need to exercise the spiritual gifts God has given us, and sensitize ourselves to the directives of His Spirit.

When we are equipped with the helmet of salvation and continually accessing the thoughts of God, we will **know** the mind of God for every situation we encounter. We do not rely on our own thoughts and puny understanding, but have access to God's divine blueprint for our lives, and clear strategies of how to **diffuse** any weapon formed against us.

> ' "**No weapon** *formed against you shall prosper, and every tongue which rises against you in judgment you will condemn. This is the heritage of the servants of the* LORD, *and their righteousness is from Me," says the* LORD.'
>
> (Isaiah 54:17)

What is real spiritual warfare?

Frequently we hear the term 'warfare' used in regard to prayer. **But there is no difference between warfare and strategic prayer**. Just as nations in battle need a strategy, God gives us strategies for prayer. While we are to be fervent and passionate in our prayer, we must remember that the devil doesn't fear teeth-gritting, fist-clenching, fist-raising, high-volume prayer. What cripples the devil and his deception is prayer that is **specific** and **strategic**. If we don't have a battle plan and a vision when praying, we are beating the air and accomplishing little.

That is why Paul talked about the necessity of connecting with a target and not merely beating the air. An army never goes to battle without a strategy or it will be guaranteed defeat. Jesus said,

> '... *what king, going to make war against another king, does not sit down first and consider whether he is able with ten thousand to meet him who comes against him with twenty thousand? Or else, while the other is still a great way off, he sends a delegation and asks conditions of peace.*'
>
> (Luke 14:31–32)

We must know what our strategy is! God has a strategy for **every** situation. No natural battle is won without a well thought-out plan, and no military leader would ever know-ingly put the lives of soldiers at risk without a winning strategy. Neither would God.

Every battle in Scripture was won **only** because people listened to God and acted on His directives (not their seemingly good ideas). We must posture ourselves to listen daily – continually. We must ask ourselves what is the mind of God in **every** situation. He will give the strategy before the attack can take place (like having an informer behind enemy lines, just as Elisha knew the Syrians plans in 2 Kings 6:12), and the devil's plans will always be diffused before they can be of any effect.

How to pray specifically in every situation

Ask the Lord specifically how to pray. He has the strategies and blueprints. We must know whom and precisely how to fight. Spiritual warfare is strategic prayer and strategic prayer **is knowing** the mind of God. We must come into alignment with His thoughts. Our goal must be accuracy in the Spirit. Getting to the heart of the matter (the mind of God) is what counts and brings results. Strategic prayer is knowing the mind of God concerning how to direct our prayer.

We are not fighting flesh and blood, but we **are** fighting.

> '*For we do not wrestle against flesh and blood, but against* **principalities**, *against* **powers**, *against the* **rulers of the darkness** *of this age, against* **spiritual hosts of wicked-ness** *in the heavenly places.'*   (Ephesians 6:12)

If we anticipate staying in a victorious posture, we must counter-plan **any** plan the enemy has devised against us. We can ask God to identify the specific names of opposing spirits, so we can stand against the devil's schemes, and crush them by binding them through aggressive prayer.

I inquired of the Lord why it was necessary to identify the names of spirits. He said, '**It gives you the edge, like having a key, otherwise you're just groping and hoping to hit something.**' We must always have a specific target to aim at, so we know precisely where to direct our prayers for maximum effectiveness, and resourcefulness of time. Remember the words of Paul:

> *'Therefore I run thus: not with uncertainty. Thus I fight; not as one who beats the air.'* (1 Corinthians 9:26)

When seeking the Lord about strategic and effective prayer, He told me,

- **'It determines what happens on earth.'**
- **'It stems the tide of change.'** Through prayer, God's hand moves and brings change in lives and in nations.
- **'It connects with the heavenlies.'** Real warfare is in the heavenly places.

> *'...against spiritual hosts of wickedness in the heavenly places.'* (Ephesians 6:12)

Specific strategy!

A few years ago, the Lord spoke clearly to my husband and me to change the way we prepare for ministry. We travel a great deal as evangelists and are in many different cities. In the past, we spent most of our time preparing for meetings, by seeking God for the **specific** topic on which to teach or preach.

But the Lord graciously instructed us to spend the bulk of our time preparing for the ministry portion of the meetings. He told us that we were to seek Him for the names of opposing or hindering demonic strongholds in each city and church in which we would be ministering; then to spend sufficient time in prayer, taking authority and dominion over the contrary spirits the Lord identifies. Now as we pray, the Lord speaks to us the names of evil spirits to rebuke, such as lethargy, lukewarmness, hard-heartedness, rebellion, skepticism, unbelief and so forth. What an adventure to spend the hours before each meeting 'tearing down' opposing spirits through prayer, and then seeing the results. Naturally, we pray ahead of time about certain topics and always come prepared and 'full' to a city.

Immediately we began to experience a much greater freedom and flow of the anointing in all our meetings and significant results followed. We noticed at once that the faith and expectancy level in the people was acutely increased (since opposing spirits were held at bay). Therefore, we see greater results in the gifts of the Spirit (healings and prophetic words, etc.), which free us not only to move in the gifts more easily, but to use less precious time exhorting people to lift their faith levels.

We have also learned that, when people come to a meeting filled with expectation and prepared to receive, the Lord will do awesome things on their behalf.

Do we spend enough time in God's presence?

Most of us believers do not spend enough time in God's presence. If we did, we would have the **answers we seek** and the **strategies we need**. We would be able to head things off at the pass, and diffuse the enemy's strategies being plotted against us, instead of wrestling and struggling with them later. **'Listening to God and communing with Him are time and trouble savers.'**

Habitually we must be sensitive to the thoughts and strategies of God (yielding up our carnal minds which are hostility against God) so precious time is never wasted in praying repetitious generalities, but **all** energy is expended toward divinely directed Holy Spirit **targets**.

> *'Therefore I run thus: not with uncertainty. Thus I fight: not as one who beats the air.'*   (1 Corinthians 9:26)

Prayer always has a **strategy** and a **divine purpose**.

Chapter 4

Practicalities of Prayer

'Canceled prayer will wear you out.'

'You can't become strong watching someone
else exercise.'

*'O God, you are My God; **early** will I seek You.'*
(Psalm 63:1)

*'My voice you shall hear in the **morning**, O Lord;
In the morning I will direct it to You, and I will look up.'*
(Psalm 5:3)

Jesus is our greatest example. He always kept His prayer
appointments with the Father. Prayer was the highest priority on His agenda. He knew that if His and the Father's
thoughts were to become one, He had to stay in sync with
Him continually through prayer.

> *'Now in the **morning**, having risen a long while before
> daylight, He went out and departed to a solitary place; and
> there He prayed.'*   (Mark 1:35)

What number is prayer on your priority list?

On one occasion while attempting to pray late in the day, but
feeling more like I was merely spinning my wheels, I casually

commented to the Lord, 'I can't seem to break through in prayer.' In the frame of mind I was in at the time (after a full day of battling every conceivable distraction that seemingly could come my way) I'm sure I was not even expecting an actual answer from the Lord. Somewhere in my puny cerebral cortex I was thinking, 'I haven't accomplished anything so far today, so I must "log in" some prayer time with the Lord before the day is totally shot.'

The Lord often chooses, what seems to us, odd times to speak some of the most profound and liberating truths. So it was that day. The Lord answered my casual question in a very loving but distinct manner through several life-changing sentences that altered my prayer life permanently. He said (referring, of course, to my comment of not being able to break through in prayer), **'Your spirit has slacked off. You must make appointments with Me and keep them. Be consistent.'** Then the finale (the six words which are now indelibly imprinted on my mind and heart): **'Canceled prayer will wear you out.'**

His penetrating words resonated in my spirit. We cannot view the highest priority in our lives (prayer and communing with God) as an option, or as something we attempt to fit into **our** schedule when it is convenient. Prayer and intimacy are as vital to the believer in keeping our spirits alive, charged, and sensitive, as oxygen is vital to keeping our bodies alive. Without consistent prayer and hearing God's voice, our hearts may easily become hardened.

> *'Today, if you will hear His voice, do not harden your hearts as in the rebellion.'* (Hebrews 3:15)

Just as soil has to be tilled before planting, our hearts have to be freshly stirred daily, or the soil of our hearts becomes hardened and crusty.

When we put off praying and spending time in the presence of the Lord, we end up fighting distractions and encountering delays throughout the day. Truly, we are worn out and little is accomplished. Consider this inspiring poem:

The Difference

I got up early one morning
And rushed right into the day;
I had so much to accomplish
That I didn't have time to pray.

Problems just tumbled about me,
And heavier came each task.
'Why doesn't God help me?'
I wondered. He answered,
'You didn't ask.'

I wanted to see joy and beauty,
But the day toiled on gray and bleak;
I wondered why God didn't show me,
He said, 'But you didn't seek.'

I tried to come into God's presence;
I tried every key in the lock.
God gently and lovingly chided,
'My child, you didn't knock.'

I woke up early this morning,
And paused before starting the day;
I had so much to accomplish,
That I had to take time to pray.   (Anonymous)

Chat room or throne room?

'Seek the LORD while He may be found, call upon Him while He is near.'   (Isaiah 55:6)

God doesn't need to find us; we need to 'find' Him daily, continually, on His terms, not ours. We should do whatever we have to do, and go wherever we have to go, in order to get **alone** with God and posture ourselves in a place where we can pray and listen **early** in the day. If we start our day dwelling on all that needs to be done (and certainly there are countless things waiting for our attention), our carnal minds will kick in and we will attempt to organize our day and shut God out of our thoughts. Conversely, if we focus on God, He will talk to us and divinely direct our day, and even multiply our time.

The devil's strategy has always been to attempt to inundate our beings with 'outside information', such as television, radio, newspapers, or even accessing the computer Chat Room instead of the Throne Room. His desire would be that we start and end our day with information that clogs our spirits. Earthly information and carnal news will kill spiritual thoughts.

Watching television, devouring a newspaper or surfing the net aren't necessarily demonic in themselves, but we miss out and even commit spiritual abortion if we make a habit of these practices (absorbing earthly input) before reading the Bible or listening to God.

The key to Kingdom accomplishments

In the first few waking moments of our day, we need to take time to listen to the Lord to hear strategies for our families and the needs of the Kingdom. The Lord has taught me that we must discipline ourselves in the first few precious minutes everyday to direct our thoughts and praise toward Him, and to inquire which hindering spirits need binding, before they can get a 'foothold' in our lives.

When I begin to pray and inquire which demonic spirits need to be bound, He often identifies several by name such as confusion, strife, anxiety, distractions, etc. Then, I immediately begin to take authority over them before the enemy can kick up any dust.

It is absolutely awesome how much God-given wealth (strategy) we can hear in a few moments if we discipline ourselves to do so, before the mind has a chance to give in to distractions. **'Listening to God is a discipline that is hard on the flesh as it contradicts the soulish desires of men.'** But, oh the joy of hearing those precious, proceeding, creative words that can engage our 'spiritual receivers' for the entire day.

God speaks at night as well

The same truth holds true of going to bed at night. Instead of letting 'Baal' (our nickname for television) or some carnal periodical leave the last imprint on our conscious minds, let us feed our spirits with God's Word, and pray that God will speak to us in the night.

> *'I will bless the* LORD *who has given me counsel;*
> *my heart also **instructs** me in the **night** seasons.'*
>
> (Psalm 16:7)

When we awaken, God will be in **all** our thoughts, and we can record the strategy and direction He speaks to us in that conveniently handy notebook at our bedside.

My husband always has a notebook by the bed (and sometimes in the bed) as he **expects** to hear God every night. More than once I have rolled over and been 'stabbed' by a pencil or pen. This ceaseless act of expectation on my husband's part to hear from God serves as a constant reminder for me to do the same. Expectancy puts a **demand** on the presence of God. God is pleased when we exhibit faith to hear. He will meet us at our level of expectancy.

> *'...without faith it is impossible to please Him.'*
>
> (Hebrews 11:6)

When we first awaken in the morning (or even in the middle of the night) we should record any dream, know-ledge, direction, etc., that we hear from the Lord. Spiritual knowledge does not come through our brains, but by the Spirit, so we may not be able to recall it later if we do not record it immediately.

If we don't understand what God has spoken, we should ask Him for interpretation. If the interpretation does not come easily, we might seek out a mature Christian and ask them to pray with us for clear understanding.

'When you pray you make room for Me'

As previously mentioned, we should do whatever we have to do and go wherever we have to go, in order to get alone with God, and position ourselves in a place where we can **pray** and **listen**. We can find our own private **place**, or take a drive, a walk, or whatever works.

If the rest of the household is awake and 'mobile' when we are trying to pray, it may become essential (though it is often difficult) to find a place of privacy. If we are determined and disciplined, God will help us make a way and find a secret place. If I am unable to find solitude at home to pray, I often resort to my 'prayer closet on wheels'. Recognizing the fact that it is not exactly safe to attempt to record God's thoughts in my journal while driving, I will often pick a comfortable spot to park (such as a safe public area). Once I am through praying I just listen and record God's specific thoughts for that day. Some people enjoy walking and praying as well.

It is not the quantity of our prayer vigil that is imperative, but the quality. If I waited until our children were raised, I might never have a prayer life. If I waited until the house was spotless, I would never have time to seek God. God does not hold us responsible for the time we do not have, but for the time we **do** have. In modern society we are all busier than ever before (even with all the newest 'time-saving' technology at our fingertips), and yet never has it been more essential to spend time with God and hear His voice.

'Seated and focused In My presence, you must inquire of Me'

I learned long ago that if you need to know something, then you must simply ask. We are encouraged to 'inquire in His temple' (see Psalm 27:4). Not only do I ask the Lord **daily** to identify hindering spirits that need binding (I have no intention of letting any unholy spirits invade any portion of our household or lives), but I have also learned to petition Him on all manner of topics on which I need answers. He is wisdom, and I need to line up with His thoughts continually. He is the One *'... in whom are hidden all the treasures of wisdom and knowledge'* (Colossians 2:3).

Many times my prayers constitute asking questions and then waiting expectantly for Him to answer. I keep asking until I feel the Spirit wane and I know God is moving on to something else. Frequently, after an intense session of prayer, I will just remain still and listen for His voice. I may hear several sentences or paragraphs of instruction or exhortation. Even when the Lord rebukes me, it is **always** edifying. If the voice we hear is not uplifting, or we feel condemnation, it probably isn't God's.

I believe one way in which many Christians are robbed, is by thinking God is only concerned with, and willing to talk about, the major goings on in our lives. After all, He is 'very busy' with so many requests. Don't be foolish. God is **as** mindful of the minute matters of our lives as He is with the paramount issues, and is willing to communicate with us on **any** issue in which clarity and direction are needed.

> *'If any of you lacks wisdom* [wants to know what God wants him to do], *let him ask of God, who gives to all* **liberally** *and without reproach, and it will be given to him.'*
> (James 1:5)

This Scripture clearly states that God is willing to give answers, but we should not merely ask for wisdom with a broad stroke in prayer, regarding **all** our needy situations, and expect an answer to **every** request all at once. If we need direction on a specific matter, we should ask God one question at a time, and wait for the answer before going on to another request.

Often in prayer times with the Lord, believers pray about a vast array of subjects and needs. We can't expect the Lord to give us one answer for all the diverse situations or petitions we've laid before Him. It's one thing to follow the direction and flow of the Holy Spirit when praying, but when listening (if the Lord has not already made the answer obvious) be sure to inquire specifically about one matter at a time.

Is all that glitters gold (God's will)?

My husband and I travel extensively as evangelists across the United States and other countries. I can honestly say in all our years of ministry we have never once (intentionally) accepted an invitation to speak or minister without **first** inquiring of the Lord if we were truly being 'sent'. God is the only One who knows if the timing is right, if the people's hearts are prepared, and if we are the instruments He has chosen to use. Ministers can literally unravel or hinder a work of the Spirit in progress if they are in the wrong place at the wrong time.

All that glitters is **not** gold. Every invitation that is extended to a minister or layman is not necessarily ordained of God. We all have flesh, and flesh (that which is not initiated by the Holy Spirit) is a hindrance to the will of God. Every seemingly good opportunity that comes into a person's life is not necessarily the divine will of God. It could very possibly be a distraction from the enemy to usurp one's time.

We must not succumb to the deception of praying whether or not something is God's will, by asking that He 'close' or 'open' the right door. That may have worked the first few weeks we were saved and still in an infantile spiritual state, but once we begin to mature in God, He **expects us** to ask Him for specific guidance and to tune in with our spiritual ears.

One minister we know encapsulated the necessity of hearing from God so profoundly. The Lord told him, 'You can learn by pain, or you can learn by listening.' And I might add that through much 'research', I recommend listening!

Chapter 5

How Prayer Works

'Vague prayers don't intimidate the devil.'

'Hearing God and praying are synonymous.'

*'The **effective, fervent prayer** of a righteous man avails much. Elijah was a man with a **nature like ours**, and he prayed earnestly that it would not rain; and it did not rain on the land for three years and six months.'*
(James 5:16–17)

Prayer should never be general, but rather specific and strategic, as the mind of the Father is being revealed continuously. '**Vague prayers don't intimidate the devil.**' People must **know** the mind of God, not formulas, clichés or parroted sermons to affect the Kingdom of God. What is received fresh from the throne through the vehicle of prayer and listening will bring life and results.

Specific and strategic prayer cripples the devil

When Elijah prayed, the heavens closed over a whole country because he **knew** both God, and the will of God. What we need is our eyes open to the possibilities of such prayer and to set ourselves to **know** God. Prayer should **always** accomplish something. It isn't meant merely to be a vehicle to release our anxieties to God, but rather to **know** the mind of God concerning our lives and the needs of the Kingdom

(Matthew 6:33), and to call forth His will in specific situations.

We serve a twenty-four-hour Holy Spirit, Who is just waiting for us to fellowship with Him and **call forth** through prayer those things which already exist in the spiritual realm. He calls things as though they already are (Romans 4:17). God speaks; we listen; we proclaim what we've heard and it manifests from its heavenly abode. The key to seeing results is **listening** for that gloriously creative, proceeding word regarding how to direct our prayers, and not merely trying to muster up some refined, legalistic, memorized confession that has no real life of God breathed into it.

Pray in the Spirit and then pray with understanding (interpretation). The Holy Spirit will bring clarity. We'll never pray the same way twice. That is precisely why we cannot limit ourselves to a mere list. Real prayer does not come out of the brain, but from our spirits. It is not cerebral, but it is birthed afresh and anew each time we pray.

Diversities of prayer

There are basically five levels in which the Spirit will direct our prayers. I have learned a great deal from our friend, Dr Mark Hanby on this area of prayer. God may guide us to flow in just one specific area, or perhaps to flow from one to another. They are:

1. **Talking to God**
2. **Praise and worship** (blessing God)
3. **Supplication** (interacting with God)
4. **Intercession** (standing between God and the situation)
5. **Travail and groanings** (birthing things out of a burden in our spirits that our conscious minds can't comprehend).

Each level is as essential as the other, but even more vital is our sensitivity to know in which area God is desiring to flow in, as **breakthroughs** in our lives will be the result. When we learn to flow in this manner daily, discerning the mind of the

Spirit, the heavens will **never** seem as 'brass' and our prayer life will take on tremendous momentum, excitement and vitality.

We cannot continue to pray in the same manner as we did in the first few months after our salvation experience. Otherwise, our prayers will be reduced to a hit and miss scenario, only occasionally hitting the mark. Once we begin to hear the Father's thoughts, we will begin to pray with greater effectiveness and confidence, knowing that **every** prayer is indeed hitting the mark and commanding an answer.

How prayer works

Here are some lessons on effective prayer that I have gradually learned over many years, and that I would like to share with you:

1. Staying up late and attempting to rise early to pray don't gel. You must be alert and attentive when communing with God. As my father-in-law likes to say, 'You can't fly with the owls at night and soar with the eagles in the daytime.' Our spiritual lives will suffer if we deny our natural bodies sufficient rest.

2. Access God's thoughts and strategies in the first few waking moments of your day. Seek God early, bind distractions and any specific hindering spirits from the enemy (which God will reveal to you if you ask), that would attempt to thwart any godly plans and purposes for your life, your family and the Kingdom of God.

3. Get **alone** with God and posture yourself in a place to pray and listen. Do not spoil the sacred holiness of your morning prayer by being noisy and distracted yourself.

4. Don't complicate prayer or attempt to reduce it to a formula, nor begin by bringing a list of your needs into the prayer closet. Be conscious of Kingdom needs first, then specific needs can follow. Yield to His direction and flow, letting Him show you first and foremost what to pray.

*'... seek first the Kingdom of God and His righteousness,
and all these things shall be added to you.'*

((Matthew 6:33)

5. Be honest, instead of religious. Don't waste precious time saying only things you think God wants to hear.

6. It is focused **quality** of prayer, not necessarily quantity which brings forth results. Many times we feel as though we have to 'log in' time with the Lord, but fervent, potent periods (of whatever duration) before the Lord with an open heart, accomplish much.

7. Pray and praise in your prayer language to find the flow of the Spirit and hear the thoughts of God. Confess what the Word says about you ('I have the health of Christ. I have the mind of Christ. No weapon formed against me shall prosper. Mountains move when I speak to them. I'm a blood-covenant person. I will bless the Lord at all times.' etc.). This helps get your 'spiritual juices' flowing. Pray and praise until you hit a 'vein' and then follow it.

8. Be sensitive to the direction and guidance of the Spirit. He will lead you. Pray in the Spirit and then pray with understanding (interpretation). Discern which area or level (as explained under diversities of prayer earlier in this chapter), God desires you to flow in and then yield to it.

9. Always have a notebook or journal, pen and flashlight (if praying with the lights off) to record what God says. Pray with anticipation. **Expect** that you will hear from God. Words from the Lord will always bypass your brain, so this necessitates recording them as quickly as possible after receiving them.

10. Prayer is a two-way conversation. Give God the opportunity to speak. Wait in His presence.

11. Be inquisitive. Ask the Lord questions. If you need to know an answer to something, ask one question at a time; then listen. Inquire specifically about what you need to know.

> *'If any man wants to know* **what God wants him to do,** *let him ask of God and God will answer liberally.'*
>
> (James 1:5 TLB)

12. If you desire enlightenment on a Scripture you've been meditating on, ask. Meditate on the Word day and night (Joshua 1:8). Carry the Word around in your spirit, 'chewing' on it until revelation is received.

    Very often, the Lord will allow a Scripture or a portion of Scripture to stand out to you. As you meditate on it, possibly for hours, days or weeks, more revelation of its meaning will flow to you from the Throne Room. It has been rightly said that idolatry is that which is foremost on your mind. Therefore, 'idolize' the Word, and God will expound and expand it to you.

Kingdom strategies for your children

I inquired of the Lord what His strategy is for children. He answered, **'Keep a vision before them.'** Then I asked, 'What is the vision?' and He spoke four things:

1. **'Spiritual maturity.'** Pray daily for spiritual hunger and God's destiny for their lives.

2. **'Teach them to use their spiritual weapons.'** Obviously prayer and spiritual authority are our greatest weapons. Sadly, praying over a meal or a repetitious bedtime prayer, are the only prayers some children are ever taught.

3. **'Teach them to utilize the gifts of the Spirit.'** Children can be trained to be sensitive to all nine gifts of the Holy Spirit (1 Corinthians 12).

4. **'Instruct them how to seek the Kingdom, and then I'll meet them.'** Teach them how to seek God and encourage them to expect to hear God's voice.

The Lord has revealed to me through the years when praying for our children, grandchildren, etc., to always pray **consistently** and **daily** for them in these areas. I have listed five specific areas He spoke to me in this regard.

1. Pray for continual spiritual hunger and an insatiable desire for the Word of God in the child (regardless of age), and for his God-ordained destiny to be fulfilled on earth. Children cannot grow spiritually on their parents' experiences with the Lord. It is imperative they have their own encounters with God.

2. Ask God which giftings He has chosen for that child's life (preferably at an early age, but it is never too late to ask), and call it forth through prayer each day.

3. Take authority daily over spirits (specific ones if He has so directed) that will no doubt attempt to hinder their walk with the Lord. Always bind any self-centeredness, rebellious spirits, lack of respect for authority, etc., which are common in most children's lives, and easily become successful tools in the hand of the enemy to 'snuff out' their spirituality. God will graciously specify if you ask for the names of precise spirits which would attempt to rob, kill or destroy your child's walk with the Lord. Pray for a 'hedge' of divine protection around them continually.

4. Pray for spiritual and uplifting peers (this is crucial). Children will often follow what peers say and do, over parental guidance. We want children to be a light to others, but not to have their light put out by rebellious and manipulative peers.

   'Do not be deceived: "Evil company corrupts good habits."'
   (1 Corinthians 15:33)

   It is paramount that our children be surrounded by other children who can encourage them in the Lord so they, in turn, can encourage others.

5. Always pray for your children's future mates, that they will be saved for each other, and that God will do the necessary 'workings' He desires in each of their lives before any marriage is consummated. Start at an early age if possible. If your child is already of dating age, or soon will be, pray that God keeps him or her out of any relationship that is not of Him. We do not live in a

fairytale world, but godly parents and grandparents **do** possess the capability to hear God and the authority to head off any ungodliness at the pass before the enemy has an opportunity to get his foot in the door. For a child's destiny to be fulfilled it is vital that he or she be united in marriage with the partner God has chosen for him or her. If your child has married out of the will of God you cannot, of course, pray against the marriage, but that God's will and purpose for that child's life, and that of his or her spouse here on earth, will be fulfilled.

Oftentimes, when praying with a parent of a rebellious child, I'll hear names of specific spirits such as delusion, darkness, evasiveness, disrespect, etc. Some spirits may be obvious, others not. That is why it is imperative to have God identify them and then head them off at the pass through prayer. Almost always, there is a rebellious peer in the picture somewhere fueling the rebellion.

Children are vulnerable to the devil, but they are also pliable to God. Until they reach a place where they can walk in authority for themselves, we must do it for them. Children can't hold up their own shields of faith without spiritual experience.

> '...above all, taking the shield of faith with which you will
> be able to quench **all** the fiery darts of the wicked one.'
>
> (Ephesians 6:16)

Children are not skilled in the ways of spiritual battle. Teach and train them how to walk and live in the Spirit.

There is no **greater gift** you could give your children, other than life itself and leading them to salvation, than to teach them how to **pray effectively** and **walk in their own God-given authority**.

Chapter 6

Let My People Grow
(*Hearing God's Voice*)

'When you begin to hear, you begin to grow.'

'The thing the devil fears the most is intimacy.'

'Intimacy brings life to your bones, cleansing to
your soul and light to your mind.'

*'All shall **know Me**,*
from the least of them to the greatest of them.'
(Hebrews 8:11)

'Man shall not live by bread alone; but man lives by every
*word that **proceeds** from the mouth of the LORD.'*
(Deuteronomy 8:3)

'Let him who glories glory in this,
*that He understands and **knows Me**.'*
(Jeremiah 9:23)

'To know Him, to know Him,
Is the cry of my heart.
Spirit, reveal Him to me.
To hear what He is saying,
Is life to my bones.
To know Him, to know Him alone.'
(A song of the Spirit given to our friend, Danny Mullins)

God never stops talking

The highest priority we must have as Christians is to seek intimacy with God. To build a relationship we must hear Him, and to hear Him we must build a relationship.

Praying effectively and according to the will of God, involves **hearing** the voice of God. How can we know what to pray if we are not hearing Him tell us what to pray?

Hearing God's voice can only be experienced in conjunction with having an open and teachable heart.

> *'Today, if you will hear His voice, do not harden your hearts.'*
> (Hebrews 4:7b)

God never stops talking. Only our ability to hear is intermittent.

Satan's first attack on humanity was an attempt to destroy all communication with our Creator. Of course, he still attempts to obstruct our hearing God through discouragement and distractions.

Man was never meant to live by bread alone, but by every fresh word that **proceeds** from the mouth of God (see Deuteronomy 8:3). God is continuously speaking and His words always carry **creative** power. One word from Him can change **any** situation. 'Peace! Be still!' quieted a potentially disastrous storm. 'Come' was the only word Peter needed to commence his supernatural 'excursion' on the water.

What keeps us from knowing You?

One day while praying, I specifically asked the Lord, 'How can we know Your power and presence?'

He answered, **'I will move through the fruitful vine.'**

I then asked, 'Who is the fruitful vine?' and the Lord responded, **'Those who have paid the price to know Me.'**

Again I asked, 'What keeps us from knowing You?'

The Lord said, **'Self-satisfaction and distractions.'**

No doubt these two areas are the greatest hindrances to our intimacy with God. When Christians become self-satisfied,

God's hands are tied, because they cease to live with a demand on His presence. God responds to our level of expectation and fervent desire.

> *'He is a rewarder of those who **diligently** seek Him.'*
> (Hebrews 11:6)

When believers are distracted, all potential fruitfulness is wasted on lesser things that have little significance for the Kingdom of God. A life-changing sentence the Lord spoke to me was, **'Distractions come in necessary-looking packages.'** Distractions can put a tourniquet around the flow of the Holy Spirit in our lives, so it is mandatory that we stay on guard against them.

Martha was performing a seemingly useful task as she was preparing a meal for Jesus. But obviously she was so over-occupied that He needed to correct her,

> *'Martha, Martha, you are worried and troubled* [distracted] *about many things. But one thing is needed, and Mary has chosen that **good part**, which will not be taken away from her.'*   (Luke 10:41–42)

Mary chose fellowship with God over the apparently demanding tasks. Obviously, she had a revelation that certain natural things would get taken care of regardless, if she made time for quality intimacy and fellowship with God. She no doubt had to resist the familiar struggle of 'the need to be needed' (performance) which we all face.

God will speak to you

There are several **keys** to hearing His voice. **The first key is to realize that, although God is supernatural, He may not be spectacular.** He often speaks in a still small voice.

> *'. . . and after the fire, a still small voice.'*
> (1 Kings 19:12)

A second key is to come before God with an attitude of expectation. A heart full of expectation 'pulls' the answer out of God.

> *'But let him ask in faith, with no doubting, for he who doubts is like a wave of the sea driven and tossed by the wind. For let not that man suppose* [expect] *he will receive anything from the Lord.'*   (James 1:6–7)

When we pray we must **believe** and know that He is going to answer us – very possibly in those next few moments.

A third key is to keep it simple. Hearing God doesn't mean we will immediately understand all kinds of divine mysteries. But the voice of the Holy Spirit will come to us to give us illumination and understanding of the specific thing we are praying about. God has a way of making profound things simple.

The fourth key is to recognize that God does not speak to the brain, but rather to the inner man. In fact, God bypasses the brain. Jesus said that out of our innermost being would flow rivers of living water (not out of our brain – see John 7:38). It is the brain that attempts to gain information instead of revelation. The brain attempts to scrutinize what God is saying and therefore aborts the flow of the Holy Spirit.

The fifth key is to expect God to be specific in talking to us. Many pray in generalities and in faithlessness. If we pray to God specifically, He will answer specifically. It is good to always keep a record of all that He says. We should do this on a daily basis. Keeping a record is an act of expectation toward God.

Okay then, how does God speak to us?

I have had the great privilege, early in my walk with the Lord, to spend time among seasoned Christians, who were not only sensitive to God but loved to seek His face. I learned from the 'adventures' of praying together with them, that the Holy Spirit is more than willing to communicate with His people. I also quickly recognized that He speaks to us in **many** different ways.

Here are some of the most apparent and frequent ways in which God speaks, learned (some the hard way) through years of seeking God:

1. **The Scriptures.** Often a certain verse will 'leap' off the page at you, as the Holy Spirit is making you **know** that this is a specific insight or direction from Him for you at that moment.

    > *'All Scripture is given by inspiration of God, and is profitable for doctrine, for reproof, for correction, for instruction in righteousness.'*   (2 Timothy 3:16)

    For example, when we were proceeding to purchase a building for our new church in Texas, it was obvious that the building would need considerable work to fit the needs of our newly formed congregation. The diversity of jobs needing professional workers was a bit overwhelming. As we were praying for direction as to whether or not we should proceed, and if so, who we were to procure for all the revamping needed, my husband opened his Bible and this verse literally 'leapt' out at him:

    > *'And David said to his son Solomon, "Be strong and of good courage, and do it; do not fear nor be dismayed, for the LORD God – my God – will be with you. He will not leave you nor forsake you, until you have finished all the work for the service of the house of the LORD ... **Every willing craftsman will be with you for all manner of workmanship, for every kind of service;** also the leaders and all the people will be completely at your command."'*   (1 Chronicles 28:20–21)

    As we proceeded to purchase the building, this Scripture was fulfilled miraculously. We stood in awe as God supplied all kinds of skilled and willing workers who volunteered their services in the following weeks.

2. **Thoughts and impressions**. A common way that God talks to us is by giving us His thoughts on a matter. Most of us have experienced having a strong thought and have dismissed it, only to realize later that it was indeed the voice of the Lord coming to us.

> *'For behold, He Who forms mountains, and creates the wind, **Who declares to man what His thought is...**'*
> (Amos 4:13)

Many of us are guilty of having our minds flooded with fruitless thoughts which clog the flow of the Spirit in us. A thought from God is **not** a part of our thinking process. When God interjects a thought into our spirits, it has nothing to do with **our** thinking or rationalization. He puts the thought into our spirits, bypassing the brain.

For example, one day in January 1986, I heard a prominent television news network talking about the space shuttle that was scheduled to be launched the following day. Suddenly, a phrase interrupted my thoughts, 'Something is going to go wrong.' Clearly this was God letting me know His thoughts, as the tragedy unfolded the following day. All I knew was that I was to pray, which I did.

3. **Hearing words in your spirit**. Often the Lord will give us a phrase in our spirits concerning what we are praying about. This will not be audible and will often be slight, almost imperceptible, yet distinct enough for us to recognize it is indeed the voice of the Lord.

> *'Your ears shall hear a word behind you, saying, "This is the way, walk in it..."'*   (Isaiah 30:21)

Of course, no word that God would speak would ever contradict Scripture, His written Word.

For example, I was praying with a dear friend who lives in another state whom I see only occasionally. We were not really praying about any particular needs, but endeavoring to follow the flow of the Spirit. Suddenly, I heard these words in my spirit concerning my friend, 'It will be like a sigh of relief to you.' She thanked me and said something to the fact that she would have to wait and see what God was referring to. But I wasn't content to leave it there. I immediately allowed my brain to kick in and assumed that the Lord was alluding to the relief it would be when my friend completed her master's degree. I quickly came to the realization that the word had nothing to do with her graduate work, when hearing a week later that she was diagnosed with a lump in her breast. Upon hearing her diagnosis, the Lord immediately reminded my friend of the previous creative word from Him, which proved to be a great source of comfort to her. After a series of tests she was given a clean bill of health and most assuredly did experience a 'sigh of relief'.

4. **Peace.** A very common way in which God talks to individual believers is through His peace. His peace guides us and He promises us that the 'peace of God' will be as an umpire in our hearts, continually leading us.

> 'And let the peace [soul harmony which comes] from the Christ rule [**act as an umpire continually**] in your hearts – deciding and settling with finality all questions that arise in your minds . . . '   (Colossians 3:15 Amp)

We must recognize the difference between having the peace **of** God and having peace **with** God. Basically, any born again believer, who loves God and desires to serve Him, has peace **with** God. This is simply part of the blood covenant. But I am referring here to a common way in which God speaks to the believer, which is through the peace **of** God (or the lack thereof) concerning specific situations.

For example, many times when someone approaches me for counsel, and the person is enthusiastically declaring some plans, it seems that my peace begins to evaporate. I know that the Guide within is telling me that the person is departing from God's will in the matter of which he is speaking.

5. **Pictures and visions**. The Holy Spirit will often graciously give pictures as we pray. The Bible tells us in Hosea 12:10 that,

> '*I have also spoken by the prophets, and have multiplied visions; I have given symbols* [similitudes] *through the witness of the prophets.*'

These similitudes (the Hebrew word *damah* meaning 'mental image') are two dimensional, as if looking at a photograph. A believer may have his eyes closed as he is praying and the Holy Spirit will give him a picture describing the answer to the subject he is praying about. A vision is three dimensional and is more rare. However, God promises to speak through visions (Acts 2:17). A similitude or picture that is given by the Spirit, could easily be described as an impression that one sees in his spirit. It can come in the form of a still picture (mental image) or a moving scene. Through the years, God has spoken to me through pictures (similitudes) more than any other way. Although they come most frequently when I am praying with my eyes closed, sometimes I will see them while in conversation or speaking prophetically, or even while teaching. These pictures are extremely accurate. Without fail, they **always** describe the situation I am praying about or about the person to whom I am prophesying.

For example, since my husband and I pray about all speaking engagements, these pictures are the most frequent way in which He reveals His will to us. When we ask the Lord if we are to accept an invitation to speak, He may speak to us by showing one or both of us a picture regarding His will. The meaning of the picture is usually obvious enough so there will be no strain in interpreting it. We may see things such as an abundance of fruit on a tree, a green light, fast-moving water (the Holy Spirit) etc. A vision is more rare, but an extremely vivid experience. One may see it with eyes wide open. In fact, it is so real that it appears as real life. The Lord lifts a veil momentarily to reveal something. Whether a vision or a picture – the source is the Lord.

6. **The word of knowledge and word of wisdom**. This has nothing to do with knowledge that is learned through studying. These gifts of the Holy Spirit are spoken about in 1 Corinthians 12:8:

> *'...for to one is given the **word of wisdom** through the Spirit, to another the **word of knowledge** through the same Spirit.'*

When the Holy Spirit speaks this way, we suddenly receive a 'knowing' in our spirits regarding something or someone. This gift is a wonderful 'tool', especially in prayer, because the Spirit is revealing precisely what to pray and how to pray. Receiving knowledge from the Lord is one of the most common ways in which we hear from Him. Just as a husband and wife seem to know one another's thoughts, we can recognize God's thoughts because of our relationship with Him. We can **know** what is on His mind as He desires to communicate with us in this way.

For example, a friend of ours who is a pastor was in dire straits over a situation in his church. He called us for prayer and wisdom. As I sought the Lord, I heard the Lord say 'six weeks'. Our friend embraced the word and took his hands off the situation. Exactly six weeks to the day from when he called, God moved and rectified the entire dilemma. God is so good!

7. **Dreams**. Many times God will give a believer a dream of guidance, instruction, encouragement, prophetic direction, or even warning. This is fairly common in Scripture. Even Joseph received a dream:

> *'Now when they had departed, behold, an angel of the Lord appeared to Joseph in a dream...'*   (Matthew 2:13)

We must recognize that in the last days God has promised to pour out His Spirit and speak to us.

'I will pour out of My Spirit on all flesh; your sons and your daughter shall prophesy, your young men shall see visions, your old men shall dream dreams.'   (Acts 2:17)

It is one thing to receive something from God; it is another thing to know what to do with it. It is always safe to take the spiritual approach. Look at anything He says as having a spiritual meaning unless He is clearly indicating otherwise.

For example, dreams about giving birth or a death are very seldom literal, although they could be on rare occasions. Giving birth almost always signifies God is birthing something fresh in our lives, and dying would most likely imply that you are dying to self (your flesh) and that your spirit is gaining momentum.

Regardless of the way in which God speaks to us, we must always be mindful to pray for interpretation. What is spiritually given, is spiritually appraised.

'These things we also speak, not in words which man's wisdom teaches but which the Holy Spirit teaches, comparing spiritual things with spiritual.'   (1 Corinthians 2:13)

Many people take a spiritual dream or vision and make it to be something natural, when indeed God is revealing a spiritual principle.

Growth comes from hearing!

If you are not experiencing God's voice in any or all of these ways in your life, then **ask** God to open your spiritual ears and ask that He begin to reveal Himself to you in whatever manner He chooses. We must train and discipline ourselves to pay attention to the Holy Spirit so the life of God can flow to us and through us.

Jesus said, *'My sheep hear My voice'* (John 10:27). Spiritual growth is inevitable when a believer begins to hear from God. There is nothing more exciting than personally hearing the Holy Spirit and then acting upon what He says. Prayer becomes a delight because communication is established, and as we hear the voice of the Holy Spirit, we experience His life.

Having our own experiences of hearing God and responding to His voice, perpetuate an exercise of spiritual stretching and quantum growth. The inner man begins to take on maturity and strength!

Chapter 7

Our Greatest Spiritual Weapon

'Praying in the spirit dispels darkness and
commands light.'

'But you shall receive **power** when the Holy Spirit has
come upon you; and you shall be **witnesses** to me in
Jerusalem, and in all Judea and Samaria,
and to the **end of the earth**.'
(Acts 1:8)

'But you, beloved, **building yourselves up** on your most
holy faith, praying in the Holy Spirit.'
(Jude 20)

Our spirit is like a battery that must constantly hold a Holy
Ghost charge (Jude 20). We cannot influence anyone else or
hope to possess the mind of the Spirit if we are not built up
ourselves. Just a small amount of corrosion on the battery
cables can keep an engine from starting and inhibit the
conduction of electricity. Similarly, if we do not pray
frequently in the spirit, we let the cares of the day 'corrode'
our connection to the Holy Spirit.

Praying in the spirit could be likened to putting meat
tenderizer on a cut of meat. The more we pray, the more
sensitive and tender our spirits become, making it possible to
hear clearly the voice of the Lord.

Additionally, praying in the spirit is a most unselfish act. How can we edify someone else, if we are not edified ourselves?

> *'He who speaks in a tongue edifies himself...'*
> (1 Corinthians 14:4)

If we are strengthened and edified through praying in the spirit, then the body of Christ, and those whose paths we cross each day, will be the benefactors. The main goal of our spiritual walk is not to seek what God can do for us, but what **we** can do to increase the Kingdom of God.

We must realize that being baptized in the Holy Spirit is not solely for our benefit, but that we might be a channel through which His life and power can flow to others. The Holy Spirit is not a 'spiritual reward' or 'stamp of approval', but a gift that our lives might be an outflow of blessing.

> *'You shall be witnesses to Me.'*   (Acts 1:8)

Yielding to the Spirit through prayer and the gifts of the Spirit, is the most unselfish thing we can do. Being on fire, getting excited, learning to hear God more clearly, and praying for a larger vision, are all unselfish actions which influence the Kingdom of God.

Don't just pray for prayer's sake – pray to **know Him**. I have found that when I pray in tongues, my priorities and thoughts come into sharper focus; my attitudes change; my 'inner man' is strengthened; my faith is increased, and God drops fresh ideas into my heart.

We must be willing to flow with Him in prayer and pursue the relationship on His terms, instead of our religious preconceptions.

What is the Christian's greatest weakness?

According to Scripture, the greatest **weakness** we have as Christians is that we do not know **how** to pray!

> *'So too the Holy spirit comes to our aid and bears us up in our weakness for we do not know what prayer to offer nor how to offer it worthily as we ought, but the Holy Spirit Himself goes to meet our supplication and pleads in our behalf with unspeakable yearnings and groanings too deep for utterance.'*   (Romans 8:26 Amp)

On the other hand, Scripture states the Christian's greatest **strength** is praying in the spirit (i.e. exercising our godly prayer language).

> *' ... building yourselves up on your most holy faith, praying in the Holy Spirit.'*   (Jude 20)

When we pray in the spirit, the Holy Spirit intercedes for us (completely bypassing our brains). Since neither our brains, nor the devil, can understand our heavenly prayer language, whatever God is desiring to accomplish through the vehicle of prayer, cannot be defiled.

The Holy Spirit bypasses the brain

One of the greatest truths I have come to know is that the analytical mind can be the Christian's greatest enemy. God is not anti-intellectual, but He doesn't need our brains to 'figure out' what He is doing. Any time God communicates to us, He is speaking to our inner man and not to our intellectual thought processes. We hear God in our spirits, and then our brains are second to know. That is why praying in the spirit is so significant, because the brain is being bypassed and our spirit is in direct communication with God.

> *'For he who speaks in a tongue does not speak to men but to God, for no one understands him; however, **in the spirit** he speaks mysteries.'*   (1 Corinthians 14:2)

Pray in the Spirit and pray with understanding

The precise reason praying in tongues is so paramount is because it helps us **focus** on our target, so we know exactly where we are going according to the Holy Spirit's guidance. The reason we pray both in the spirit and with understanding (interpretation) is because it helps us make the connection in our **mind** (see 1 Corinthians 14:14–15). We must always know **where** we are going spiritually, what hindering demons we are addressing and what is the will of God that needs to be accomplished through our prayers at that particular moment.

When praying in tongues, we are not only sensitizing our spirits to hear from God, but we are sending out a 'spiritual signal' to connect with God's will and purpose for that time. When we pray with the spirit **and** with the understanding, we are seeking divine direction, like radar (the Holy Spirit makes intercession for us – Hebrews 7:25), and when He comes back with direction, He has already searched the deep things of God and will bring back an interpretation of our prayer.

If we pray in the spirit solely, never making the connection with what God desires to accomplish through prayer at that precise moment, then we may well be coming short of hitting the God-ordained mark that He has intended.

We must initiate praying in the spirit; then God speaks; then we acknowledge what He has spoken (after hearing God's thoughts), which generates tremendous spiritual momentum. We can then yield to His flow and inevitably **His will is accomplished**. The increase of the Kingdom of God is the direct result as we 'birth forth' His will on earth.

> *'Your Kingdom come, Your will be done on earth as it is* [already declared] *in heaven.'*　　　　　(Matthew 6:10)

Additionally, hindering demons have been identified, bound, and rendered helpless, leaving them no leverage to thwart the will and purpose of God for our lives.

Robbery and attempted assault versus pure unadulterated intercession

There are occasions when God chooses not to reveal the target of our prayers (usually for reasons obvious later), yet

He will give knowledge in our spirits that accomplishment or victory is imminent or being done as we pray.

On one occasion I felt a great burden for our son, David, which would not cease. For several weeks I literally wept and prayed incessantly in the spirit for him. The Lord did not reveal to me why I was continually in this vigil of intercession, but I knew in my spirit something serious from the devil's plate was being diverted.

Really, you would think the devil would be shrewd enough not to pick on our beloved children. He knows all too well that there is no one meaner than a woman provoked. Or my rendition would be, there's nothing that makes a praying mother more aggressive then when her child is being attacked (like a mother bear and her cubs).

At the time David was just seventeen and in his junior year in high school. Everything seemed to be going smoothly in his life. After all, he was attending a wonderful Christian school; most of his friends were 'sold out' to God; and thankfully, David himself possessed his own wealth of godly passion and hunger for the things of the Spirit.

Then came the robbery. In broad daylight in a section of our city thought by many to be safe, he and his friend were robbed at gun point by four men. All the perpetrators were armed and had the audacity to point their dastardly firearms in the face of our 'angelic' son. This all occurred within a few moments, as a large white van came, seemingly out of nowhere, screeched to a halt in the middle of the street, stopping directly in front of them, and the men wielding firearms appeared and took aim.

Thanks be to God, no one was injured. The boys wisely yielded up their wallets upon demand; the van door slammed shut, and the four robbers sped off at a high speed. David and his friend were left standing in the street (in a mild state of shock), trying to assimilate what had just transpired.

'Reign' on the devil's parade

The news quickly made its way to my husband and me. At first, I was so mad I thought of David (in the Bible) when he fearlessly overcame the lion and the bear, defeating them single-handedly (1 Samuel 17); or when he challenged Goliath, declaring, 'Who is this uncircumcised Philistine, that he should defy the armies of the living God?' (or the son of a praying mother). For a few fleeting moments I thought, 'I'll go hunt those thieves down myself.' Then reality set in and my anger and temporary insanity turned to pure thanksgiving unto God, as the fact sank in that God had graciously spared both boys from any harm. They were now perhaps, a little more street wise, but nonetheless unharmed. Even our son's wallet (found empty) was later returned by an honest citizen with his driver's license still in it.

Of course, the purpose of the intense burden for intercession for our son was quite obvious now. And no doubt, my prayers were just a drop in the bucket compared to those of all the others God most assuredly moved on to pray for David and his friend.

Since God chose not to give me the knowledge at the beginning of why I was praying for him, the gift (or tool) of praying in the spirit was the greatest weapon I could utilize. The prayers that went forth literally created a 'canopy' of divine protection. Coincidentally, the heavy burden I could not shake before, was now gone.

The Bible says of those who choose to make God's presence their dwelling place,

> 'He shall call upon Me, and I will answer him; I will be with him in trouble; I will deliver him and honor him.'
>
> (Psalm 91:15)

Truly, our greatest spiritual weapon is the gift of praying in the spirit, which enables us to **know** the mind of God in **every** situation.

No lion shall be there – a place of safety

There is a place in God where we can live above all earthly pulls and demonic ploys. God has a highway built for us, but there are conditions required to travel on it.

*'A highway shall be there, and a road [walk], and it shall be
called the **Highway of Holiness**. The unclean shall not pass
over it. But it shall be for others. Whoever walks the road,
although a fool [wayfaring man], shall not go astray. **No
lion shall be there, nor shall any ravenous beast go up
on it; it shall not be found there**. But the **redeemed** shall
walk there.'*
                                                    (Isaiah 35:8–9)

The Highway of Holiness is a place in our walk with the
Lord that we can attain to by walking in righteousness and
holiness and staying ever sensitive to any demonic schemes
with which the devil would attempt to gain entrance to our
lives, seeking to throw us off our footing. By staying on guard
(watchful in prayer), taking authority over specific spirits
which the Lord will identify if we ask, and living a godly life,
we can be assured of His protection (with the absence of
Satan's ploys) on His highway.

The devil (roaring lion) and his demonic hoards (ravenous
beasts), can not go up on it (the Highway of Holiness), but
only about it.

*'Be sober, be vigilant; because your adversary the devil walks
about like a roaring lion, seeking whom he may devour.'*
                                                    (1 Peter 5:8)

The enemy can only attack those who turn off the way of
holiness. Protection comes in the secret place:

*'He who dwells in the secret place of the Most High shall
abide under the shadow of the Almighty.'*   (Psalm 91:1)

You may hear the devil's roar, but you won't feel the bite.
If you veer from the highway, you may feel the bite if you
don't repent. Holiness is a walk of the Spirit. The unclean
(unrighteous, apathetic, unholy) shall not walk on the highway.

If we want to experience the anointing that breaks every
yoke we must love righteousness and hate iniquity (see

Hebrews 1:9). We can't walk successfully where there is uncleanness in our lives. The pure in heart will 'see' God.

> '*Pursue peace with all people, and holiness, without which no one will **see** the Lord.*'   (Hebrews 12:14)

The fool, or wayfaring (way-transgressing) person, is one who is not sensitive to the Spirit. They will have a difficult time walking a straight path on the highway.

To travel on God's highway necessitates a walk of holiness and righteousness, and a continual desire to 'see the Lord' (staying sensitive through prayer), walking uprightly.

> '*For it would have been better for them not to have known the way of righteousness, than having known it, to turn from the holy commandment delivered to them.*'   (2 Peter 2:21)

God is challenging all of us to come up higher. His desire is that all believers ascend to that place in the Spirit, where we can choose to stay in continual communion with Him. And that we discipline ourselves (ever sensitive and aggressive to Satan's schemes) to walk in a worthy manner (above all earthly circumstances), remaining on the Highway of Holiness.

Chapter 8

Never Let the Devil See You Sweat

'Don't converse with evil spirits, push them back.'

> *'Therefore submit to God.*
> ***Resist** the devil and **he will flee** from you.'*
> (James 4:7)

The Lord is training us to respond **only** to His voice and to stay continually sensitive to the enemy's tactics. **'If you keep your spiritual** (parking) **meter "plugged" you won't be ticketed by the enemy. If he "targets" you, it won't be effective because divine intervention will have already been put into motion. The devil can't touch a full tank.'** The Bible clearly says,

> *'Walk in the Spirit* [be fully under His influence] *and you shall not fulfill the lust of the flesh.'*   (Galatians 5:16)

Many mistakenly get into a conversation with the devil. **'Don't converse with evil spirits, push them back.'** Ephesians 4:27 confirms, *'Neither give place to the devil'*.

We must live on the offensive and be aggressive toward all the wiles of the devil (Ephesians 6:11), with a prayer life that prevents any demonic strategy from gaining a foothold.

Most Christians live too passively as far as their prayer lives are concerned and therefore let the enemy walk on them, instead of the opposite. We are to tread on him.

*'Behold, I give **you** the authority to trample on serpents and scorpions, and over all the power of the enemy, and nothing shall by any means hurt you.'*   (Luke 10:19)

'You are not the servant of evil spirits. Don't let any unholy spirits take you hostage or invade your household. Attack them.'

Little foxes with large appetites

There is an extremely significant scripture that says,

'Catch us the foxes, the little foxes, that spoil the vines; for our vines have tender grapes.'   (Song of Solomon 2:15)

The Lord revealed to me that the little foxes are anything that takes our focus off the Spirit and gets it on the flesh. I said, 'Lord, please be more specific.' He then said, '**Frustrations, irritations, strife, anxiety, worry, negative thoughts and negative words that come at you through others.**'

There is no question that evil spirits ride in on the words that people speak. It is so easy to get our focus off the Spirit and get in the flesh by becoming irritated and burdened down, resulting in our joy being robbed. When our joy is stolen, our peace goes, our strength goes, and everything else seems to go with it.

Grapes (*'for our vines have tender grapes'*) are used to make wine, and wine is always indicative of the joy of the Lord. It is the little foxes that rob our joy. It is not the monumental things that come into our lives that rob our joy, because we are more readily braced for them.

Catch those foxes

God commands **us** to **catch** the little foxes. He is saying, 'I've given you the strategy and authority you need to head these things off at the pass.' Strategic prayer is not **after the fact** (or praying after the problem manifests), rather it is praying and taking authority **before** the little things take root and the foxes have an opportunity to rip us off.

God has made clear the strategy, that every single day upon rising, we can ask the Lord how to pray and what to come against. Ask God for the names of specific spirits trying to rob you, your family members and so forth. You will be amazed how the foxes won't have **any place** in you whatsoever, since you have already taken authority over their influence.

Actually, most of the prayers we pray are after the fact, namely, after the situation has already occurred; after the sickness has come; after the problems surface. Then we pray against the symptom. But God says He has given **us** the strategy to head them off at the pass. The sickness, problem, and deception can't find a lodging place and germinate, because strategic prayer has been in operation. Therefore, we must get our focus on the Lord and His plan early in the day. We want God to catch the foxes, but God says, 'No, **you catch** them.' He will give the strategies and specifics, but we must **take** the Kingdom by force.

> '...*The kingdom of heaven suffers violence, and the violent take it by force.'*   (Matthew 11:12)

Passivity never accomplishes anything, but passionate and aggressive prayer will get the job done.

If we knew a burglar was targeting our home, we would take all necessary precautions. Never let the devil trespass on your property. Access God's thoughts and directives and utilize your God-given authority.

Work hardest on known weaknesses

The Lord began to speak to me to acknowledge my greatest areas of weakness, and to pray for strength and growth in those areas so the enemy would have no leverage against me. We are **never** to give place to the devil in any area, but we should work especially hardest on those areas we **know** are a weakness in us.

For example, if I am a person who has a problem with being late, I need to seek the Lord for grace and help in that area. It is crucial, because the enemy sees the weakness and takes full advantage of it, by using it to cause frustration and anger in others, to ruin my testimony, etc. In other words, I need to work hardest on the weakest area so the enemy has no access. As we choose to overcome weaknesses, those areas become our greatest strengths. For instance, if a weak or defective part of a machine is replaced, that new part is now the strongest part of the machine. Jesus said,

> '... *for the ruler of this world is coming, and he has **nothing** in Me.'* (John 14:30)

Taking authority over more foxes

When our son was around twelve years old, we noticed him becoming somewhat depressed and melancholic. Soon he expressed an attitude of not wanting to go to church with us and was avoiding the spiritual conversations to which our family was accustomed. Needless to say, we began to pray and access the Holy Spirit on what to do. He made it clear to my husband and me that we must pray aggressively and take authority over the devil who was harassing him. As we prayed, the Lord spoke to us the name of specific evil spirits to bind that had found access to our son's ears.

I remember binding spirits such as depression, heaviness, melancholy, lukewarmness, apathy, distortion and spiritual blindness. Within a week, our son began to change so drastically that he approached my husband and asked him if he would mind buying him a new Bible. My husband felt like buying him a dozen.

From that point in time, our son's hunger for God began to grow, and although there were occasions when we would observe him beginning to succumb to those familiar symptoms, we would immediately begin to pray against the opposing spirits and he would quickly snap back.

Obviously, this was a great spiritual lesson for us as parents and taught us to always stay on our spiritual toes (aware and sensitive to any divisive spirits), and to be quick to stop (in its tracks) any scheme of the enemy being plotted against any of our children.

If you insist on carrying burdens, God cannot

'Prayer is divine. Worry is demonic.' Worry is tantamount to handing the devil an invitation to rob us blind. We only become prey when Satan senses any vulnerability in us. If we give him 'no place', then he has no place to invade. If we resist him he **will** flee from us. Leave no place and he'll gain no ground. We must not give the devil ammunition by succumbing to worry. 'Burdens are not wholesome.' The devil continually wants to keep us on the edge in stress, strain and strife, instead of remaining carefree by trusting and abiding in God. But we must never let the devil see us sweat.

The vision (the attaché altar)

The Lord gave me a liberating vision regarding worry that changed my prayer life permanently. I'm sure it was no coincidence that at the time of this visitation, I was under a weighty circumstance which I was attempting to walk through, instead of having victory over.

I would, of course, go to the Lord daily for wisdom regarding this circumstance, asking Him how to pray for victory, as well as identifying (and taking authority over) any specific hindering spirits. The Lord was always gracious to give me wisdom on how to pray and what evil spirits to bind. So why did I still feel like pond scum?

Praying passionately was not my problem, but never fully releasing the circumstance to Him was. I was determined to drag the 'dead pig' (a nickname we called an old vacuum cleaner we once owned) around with me everywhere I went, like an unnecessary knapsack of heavy, useless rocks, never realizing I was the main deterrent to divine intervention.

Then the Lord **opened** my 'spiritual' eyes. In the vision I was kneeling at a church altar crying out to God fervently and passionately regarding the circumstance. When I ceased praying, still feeling heavy hearted, I stood up and began to fold up the rather long, but narrow altar. I kept folding and folding, as if it were made out of sheets of perforated paper, until it appeared to be the approximate size of an attaché case. Next, I simply picked up the altar like one would a briefcase and walked away with it.

The Lord's voice was abundantly clear. He spoke, '**If you insist on carrying this burden, I can't.**'

I caught on quickly. I immediately revisited that heavenly altar and released that burdensome circumstance to Him once and for all. At that very instant I not only felt as though God was engulfing me with His divine peace and presence, but joyously experienced the invisible knapsack of weighty rocks supernaturally lifted off me.

No, the circumstance didn't change overnight, and yes I still had to fervently press in to God, but I was at last free of carrying what didn't belong to me.

Today, with a heart full of thanksgiving, I can testify that God moved over and above what I expected Him to do in the first place in that particular circumstance, once the burden was left in God's hands. Pray without ceasing, but **cease** to worry about what or for whom you are praying.

Can worry make you sick?

How many loved ones can you carry in an attaché altar (without caving in from the weight)? Zero would be God's preference. We are exhorted by Peter to cast **all** our care upon the Lord for He cares for us (see 1 Peter 5:7). If we insist on yielding to worry and holding on to our burdens, never quite releasing them to God completely, then the 'dead pig' will remain our constant companion and God's hands will remain tied. The 'little foxes' will continue to sap our joy and strength.

> '*Be **anxious for nothing**, but in everything by prayer and supplication with thanksgiving let your requests be known to God.*'   (Philippians 4:6)

If anxiety is carried and not released, it may eventually wreak havoc in you through any array of physical or emotional maladies, not to mention being robbed of God's divine peace that passes all understanding. '**Care and peace cannot coexist.**' When care moves in, peace moves out.

God never implies to cease being fervent in pressing in for needs, but He is clearly saying it is not your job to **carry** them around. We must live in full assurance that He is abundantly able to conquer **any** need that could possibly arise in our lives. Ding dong, the pig is not only dead, but buried.

God's wisdom regarding loved ones

Since one of the most effective onslaughts the enemy (foxes) can perpetuate against us is to target those closest to us, I felt compelled to share some direct life-changing quotes from the Lord that He has graciously spoken to me over many years regarding loved ones. I pray they will help liberate you as much as they have me.

- '**The enemy uses loved ones to get to you as he rides in on words they speak.**'
- '**Don't take it personally – take it to Me.**'
- '**Be confident in what you know. Don't react, but grow.**'
- '**New mercies are for you every day, but you have to embrace them.**'
- '**Perfect scenarios in life don't exist – there are some things you must accept and just get on with life.**'
- '**I never promised you a rose garden ... I just promised I'd make a way.**'
- '**Fairy tales don't exist – neither do perfect people.**'
- '**Don't listen to or embrace anything negative.**'
- '**Guard your mouth as poison causes damage.**'
- '**Don't keep saying how hard it is and trying to change your loved ones for your sake, but pray they**'

will be changed for My sake and the sake of the Kingdom of God.'

- Regarding children: 'Your kids are mine, too. Don't you think I'm working on them? My grace is sufficient for you – it covers it all.'

In all this, God is obviously not implying we are not to care, or pray or speak sobering truth when needed, but He is clearly saying we must be delivered out of and above carnal situations (by viewing them through spiritual eyes) before we can conquer through the Spirit. 'The carnal drags you into the abyss, but the Spirit takes you to the mountain top.'

If you stay tuned in to God and flow in His directives, worry won't have any place in you. Then the enemy (foxes) will have no foothold, and you will live and walk in victory and the devil will never see you sweat.

Chapter 9

Thankfulness is Where Your Breakthrough Begins!

'A thankful heart is a fertile heart.'

'Continue earnestly in prayer,
*being vigilant in it with **thanksgiving**.'*
(Colossians 4:2)

In our first year of pastoring, we felt strongly to teach the people how to worship God in the Spirit. During an awesome worship session one Sunday morning, I experienced an open vision. With my eyes open I beheld two huge angels standing on both sides of the altar, holding large purple velvet pouches. As the praises were emanating from the people, musical notes were filling the atmosphere and dancing in perfect precision to a seemingly heavenly 'beat' as the notes entered into the pouches. It was obvious to me that the praises were being received and gathered to be presented to God. I'll never forget that experience. It is still just as fresh in my mind as it was many years ago.

'But you are holy, enthroned in the praises of Israel.'
(Psalm 22:3)

Thankfulness prepares us to receive from God

There is nothing that pleases God more than a thankful person. In order to receive from God we must be like fertile ground. **Rejoicing and being thankful open up our hearts to receive from God!** Nothing is more gratifying than being around a thankful person. Just as it motivates us to want to do more for a person that is thankful, so too God responds to a thankful heart. He exhorts us to pray with thanksgiving. 'Continue earnestly in prayer, being vigilant in it **with thanksgiving.**'

Fervency in our prayer life is essential, and our spiritual walk needs to abound in thanksgiving.

> '... *rooted and built up in Him and established in the faith, as you have been taught, abounding in it with* **thanksgiving.**'
> (Colossians 2:7)

From barrenness to fruitfulness

Isaiah tells the barren one to rejoice:

> '"*Sing, O barren, you who have not borne! Break forth into singing, and cry aloud. You* **who have not labored** *with child! For* **more** *are the children of the desolate than the children of the married woman,"* says the Lord.'
> (Isaiah 54:1)

When we are thankful and rejoicing, God is able to take our barrenness and turn it into fruitfulness. Notice that He spoke not to the fruitful one, but to the barren, promising that **breaking forth into rejoicing** would cause fruitfulness to manifest.

When the angel Gabriel spoke to young Mary, the first thing He told her was to **rejoice** (Luke 1:28). When we rejoice, God is able to overshadow us by the Holy Spirit and cause something to be **conceived** in us.

Rejoicing is such a vital key, because it enables us to become fertile ground and good soil, so God can plant His vision and purpose in us.

This is such an important principle. God moves in His people the same way He brought Christ into the world. He found Mary, a willing and teachable vessel, and He birthed

His purpose in her. Mary's response was the same response we should have toward the Lord at all times.

> *'Let it be unto Me according to Your word.'*   (Luke 1:38)

Don't quench the Spirit by complaining

When we cease to give thanks to God in **all** things, whether they are to our liking or not, we quench the Spirit and prevent Him from intervening on our behalf.

> *'In **everything** give thanks; for this is the will of God in Christ Jesus for you. Do not quench the Spirit.'*
> (1 Thessalonians 5:18–19)

Prayers and supplications must be accompanied with thanksgiving or they will become nullified. Being anxious, worried and weighed down with cares, is assuming a responsibility that God never gave us. When we are tempted to complain, we can command ourselves to name things we are thankful for. The list will be long.

The first generation of Israelites who left Egypt never entered into their inheritance (the promised land) because of unbelief, murmuring and complaining. That is when God declared,

> *'How long shall I bear with this evil congregation who **complain against Me?** I have heard the complaints which the children of Israel make against Me. Say to them, "As I live," says the LORD, "just as you have spoken in My hearing, so I will do to you."'*   (Numbers 14:27–28)

Equally, if we do not cease to complain, we will never get out of our present realm and into that which God has for us.

On the other hand, praise not only glorifies God, but He inhabits (is enthroned in) them.

> *'He inhabits the praises of His people.'*   (Psalm 22:3 KJV)

Thankfulness frees us from prison

When Paul and Silas were thrown in prison with their hands and feet in stocks, they began to sing praises to God. Although it would have been a 'perfect' time to grumble and complain, they **chose** instead to sing. The other prisoners heard them. When we are thankful, others take notice. That time of thankfulness released God to move, causing an earthquake which resulted in everyone's chains breaking. Our thankful attitude not only frees us, but frees **others** under our influence.

> '*But at midnight Paul and Silas were **praying and singing hymns** to God, and the **prisoners were listening** to them. Suddenly there was a great earthquake, so that the foundations of the prison were shaken; and immediately all the doors were opened and **everyone's** chains were loosed.*'
> (Acts 16:25–26)

Everyday we are surrounded by 'prisoners' of this world's system and thinking. If we choose to live with an attitude of thankfulness, God will use us to bring freedom to them.

There is no question that people closely observe believers and how they react to situations. They want to see if we believe and live what we preach. The world desperately needs to see victory in us.

Praise ushers in His presence

Three kings joined in a mission to fight against King Moab, but encountered trouble when they ran out of water for the army and their animals. The King of Israel was ready to concede defeat:

> '*Alas! For the* Lord *has called these three kings together to deliver them into the hand of Moab.*' (2 Kings 3:10)

But Jehoshaphat, the king of Judah, called for a prophet, hoping that the prophet would have the word of the Lord for them.

A servant informed Jehoshaphat about the prophet Elisha. Hearing that '*...the word of the* LORD *is with him*' (2 Kings 3:12), Jehoshaphat, along with the kings of Israel and Edom, went to seek Elisha out and consult with him. Elisha was not exactly happy to see them, and rebuked them,

> '*What have I to do with you? Go to the prophets of your father and the prophets of your mother.*'   (2 Kings 3:13)

He was obviously angry that they had sought only other gods in the past. However, because of Jehoshaphat's reputation, he decided to help.

But before he could prophesy the word of the Lord he said,

> '*"But now bring me a musician." Then it happened,* **when** *the musician played, that the hand of the* LORD *came upon him.*'   (2 Kings 3:15)

Before the prophet could function, he had to enter in to a time of **thankfulness and praise**, so he called for a musician. So many times we are in such a state of strife and frustration (Elisha was frustrated with them), that the only way we can receive direction from the Lord is to stop and surrender with worship, gratitude and thanksgiving to Him.

Then the Word of the Lord came,

> '*Thus says the* LORD: *"Make this valley full of ditches." For thus says the* LORD: *"You shall not see wind, nor shall you see rain; yet that valley shall be* **filled** *with water, so that you, your cattle, and your animals may drink."*'
>
> (2 Kings 3:16–17)

God fulfilled His word quickly as the following morning water **suddenly** filled the land. The Moabites thought it was blood, and that the kings had slaughtered one another. When they came to reap the 'spoils' Israel arose and defeated them. The word through the prophet Elisha brought victory, but it all began when the musician played, and the Spirit of the Lord came upon him. A heart of worship and thankfulness opens up the heavens.

Following are some wonderful truths that the Lord has given to me through the years regarding thankfulness.

Thankfulness:

1. **Decentralizes self.**
2. **Develops humility.**
3. **Preserves mental health.**
4. **Brings release to your inner man.**
5. **Is like medicine – it edifies the soul.**
6. **Means a thankful heart, which is a healthy heart.**
7. **Enables you to focus on Kingdom motives.**
8. **Helps you maintain reverence (keeps the things of the Spirit from becoming common).**
9. **Helps you become 'airborne' rising above obstacles.**
10. **Goes a long way – all the way to the Throne.**

Thankfulness and expectation are the keys that unlock the storehouse of heaven and open the way for God to speak to us. When God talks, awesome things always occur. **Live** with expectation. **Pray** with expectation. **Listen** with expectation.

> *'It is good to give thanks to the* Lord, *and to sing praises to Your name, O Most High; to declare Your lovingkindness in the morning, and your faithfulness every night.'*
>
> (Psalm 92:1–2)

Chapter 10

Heavenly Rewards

'Eternally, you are forever building crowns and spiritual rewards.'

'Spiritual riches in men will win the world.'

'Spend your energy on My Kingdom, not yours.'

'Trials and seasons come and go,
but Kingdom building remains.'

'I have rewards that can't be taken away and
fruit that will never spoil.'

*'For no other foundation can anyone lay than that which is laid, which is Jesus Christ. Now if anyone builds on this foundation with gold, silver, precious stones, wood, hay, straw, **each one's work will become clear**; for the Day will declare it, because it will be **revealed by fire**; and the fire will **test** each one's work, of what sort it is. If anyone's work which he has built on it endures, he will receive a **reward**. If anyone's work is burned, he will suffer loss; but he himself will be saved, yet so as through fire.'*
(1 Corinthians 3:11–15)

As I was reading this portion of Scripture, I experienced an intense 'breaking' in my spirit and began to weep. It has become apparent through the years, that when I have this type of experience, I am to remain sensitive and focused in the Lord's presence, as I know divine revelation will begin to flow from Him.

I felt impressed to focus in on verses 13–15 and ask for a deeper understanding of their meaning. My first question to the Lord was, 'Which of men's works will endure for eternity?'

He answered, '**Only those which were Spirit-initiated.**'

I pressed on and asked, 'Which of men's works will be burned?'

The Lord said, '**Those that were created through men's minds. Those that are the consequence of reasoning.**'

I continued, while attempting to absorb the awesome truths I was hearing, 'How can we recognize an "enduring" (eternal) work?'

His answers (or questions, actually) penetrated to my very core:

- '**Did you pay the price?**'
- '**Is Spirit-life breathed into it?**'
- '**Did you yield to your own initiative?**'

Many seemingly 'good works' are only wood, hay and stubble in God's eyes because the motivation behind them is not pure.

The pressures of life make us focus on the present with little thought for the eternal. Christians need to realize that how they live on the earth will determine what degree of reward they will experience in heaven.

> '*Look to yourselves, that we do not lose those things worked for but that we receive a **full reward**.*'   (2 John 8)

The Judgment Seat of Christ indicates that believers will not be judged concerning their destination, but concerning the **rewards** they will **enjoy** throughout eternity.

> '*For we must all appear before the judgment seat of Christ, that each one may receive the things done in the body, according to that he has done, whether good or bad.*'
> (2 Corinthians 5:10)

This judgment is based on the good and bad things done in the body. The good things will increase rewards; the bad things, although forgiven, will decrease them.

This means that our **eternal reward** will be determined by this present life. This is a sobering thought. What makes it even more sobering is the fact that our rewards will not be determined solely by the many good things each Christian has done. The determination will be for **every** work, whether it is good or bad.

One comforting thought about the fire test at Christ's tribunal: our good works will be purified by the **same** fire which destroys our bad works.

> '...*each one's works will become clear; for the Day will declare it, because it will be revealed by fire; and the fire will test each one's work, of what sort it is.'*
>
> (1 Corinthians 3:13)

Rather than discouraging me from my pursuit of godliness, this knowledge produces in me a sort of holy vengeance. I want to run the rest of my race with patient perseverance in pursuit of the holiness of God.

The flesh or the Spirit?

On one occasion after an intense flow in prayer, I was meditating on what it might be like to stand before the Judgment Seat of Christ and give account for the works I have rendered. Suddenly, I was experiencing a vision before my eyes in which I saw two mountains, one much larger than the other.

One mountain was huge, and I could not see around it. It had giant letters around the bottom spelling 'F-L-E-S-H.' Then, as I studied the smaller mountain (more like a hill, actually), which was dwarfed by the huge one, I saw at its base the letters, 'S-P-I-R-I-T.' I was amazed at the difference in size of the two mountains. I know that, from God's perspective, many of **our works** will end up on the flesh mountain.

Therefore, believers need a holy fear of God – a realization that all we do in this life has **eternal repercussions**. Every work will either be a product of the Spirit or the flesh. Thank God for His grace.

> '...*let us have* **grace** *by which we may serve God* **acceptably** *with reverence and Godly fear.'* (Hebrews 12:28)

Works of eternal or temporary significance?

Paul was given much insight into the believer's judgment. He distinguished the works of believers into two categories: simply that which was good and which was bad (2 Corinthians 5:10). He described them as being like gold, silver, and precious stones (good works), or like wood, hay, and stubble (bad works). Many of the good works believers perform now will be clearly seen for what they are at the Judgment Seat of Christ.

Every Christian has both good and bad works. All his works will be put to the test of fire. The works which are plainly revealed as precious jewels speak of those things done throughout life which had **eternal significance** (Spirit-life breathed into them). The wood, hay, and stubble speak of those things which had only a **temporary significance**. Although they may have looked good at the time, they were a consequence of man's reasoning, and therefore, **a product of the flesh, not the Spirit**.

Character and behavior matter. Faithfulness in one's station in life, and in every area of one's responsibilities and relationships, carry eternal rewards. Everything in life is to be done heartily as to the Lord, not to man, knowing that it is He who will reward us as well as repaying every wrong-doer without partiality. That is why Paul insists that,

> '...*whatever you do,* **do it heartily**, *as to the Lord and not to men, knowing that from the Lord you will receive the* **reward of the inheritance**; *for you serve the Lord Christ. But he who does wrong will be repaid for what he has done, and* **there is no partiality**.' (Colossians 3:23–25)

Any work performed for the glory of God never goes unnoticed by His caring eyes nor unrewarded by His generous hands. Even a cup of cold water, given in His name, will be eternally recompensed, and every **idle word** shall be accounted for (see Matthew 10:42; 12:36–37).

The compensations of **eternal rewards** will far outweigh the difficulties endured on earth.

> *'For I consider that the sufferings of this present time are **not worthy** to be compared with the **glory** which shall be revealed **in us**.'* (Romans 8:18)

How does prayer fit into eternity?

Eternal compensation will be accrued to our heavenly account to the degree that **we** choose to yield and obey God while on this earth. We can live to gratify the flesh and its desires, or we can **choose** to gratify God and carry our fruitfulness with us into eternity. God is clearly entreating us to be willing to pay the price spiritually by letting Him have His way in us, that we might become vessels of honor useful for the Master.

> *'Therefore if anyone cleanses himself from the latter, he will be a vessel for honor, sanctified and useful for the Master, prepared for every good work.'* (2 Timothy 2:21)

This means walking and living in obedience and staying sensitive to His divine directives. Are the 'works' we do a consequence of our own reasoning, initiatives and egos, or do we allow the Spirit to initiate what needs to be accomplished for His purpose? We must continually lay down our agenda that His Kingdom building can be done.

God once gave me a **life-changing** dream. In it I was in a large Christian gathering where many people were milling around and chatting. Someone walked up to me and said, 'Would you please go to the platform, as I know you have a word from the Lord for us.' My flesh didn't want to go, yet in my spirit I knew this person had heard from God. I didn't have a clue what I was going to say, but I knew I must obey the Lord.

As I began to speak, very little attention was being paid to my words, **until** I started exhorting about prayer. The moment I did, the anointing immediately intensified. With all eyes now focused on me, I said with so much godly authority it almost frightened me,

> '**It makes no difference if any of us ever stand behind a pulpit, hold a strategic office in a church, or are known for any "special" ministry.**'

I continued,

> '**Prayer is the main call on all our lives. We cannot afford to be self-centered and only think of ourselves. We must be an encouragement to others and look for those with needs, and birth forth the Kingdom of God on earth through the vehicle of prayer.**'

It was crystal clear what God was saying through the dream. Prayer is the **highest priority** on His agenda. Giving ourselves to prayer, along with obedience to the Lord, and the pouring out of our lives into others, will have eternal significance.

When Elijah was sent to the desperate widow in need, his first question to her was, *'Tell me, what do you have in the house?'* (2 Kings 4:2). Her reply was, *'Your maidservant has nothing in the house but a jar of oil'* (we always seem to emphasize 'nothing'). He instructed her to gather some empty vessels:

> *'Go, borrow vessels from everywhere, from all your neighbors – empty vessels; do not gather just a few.'*   (2 Kings 4:3)

Then she was instructed to go back in her house, shut the door behind her (to unbelief, and to obey God without conducting interviews), and then to pour the oil into all the vessels. The prophet released her from her 'prison' of fear and lack. She had stopped pouring, and using the oil (the Holy Spirit) in her house (life). The **key** to always having something fresh is to **never stop pouring out**. We must always look for empty vessels to pour our oil (the Holy Spirit) into through prayer and ministering to individuals.

> *'Now it came to pass, when the vessels were full, that she said to her son, "Bring me another vessel." And he said to her, "There is not another vessel." So the oil **ceased**.'*
>
> (2 Kings 4:6)

The **lack** of vessels (outlets) causes the oil to stop flowing.
   Finally, Elisha told her,

> *'Go, sell the oil and pay your debt; and you and your sons live on the rest.'*   (2 Kings 4:7)

We will never lack in our lives as we continue to pour out.

The harvest

One day while in prayer, the Lord spoke to me, **'If the laborers aren't strong the harvest will be spoiled.'**

> *'Then He said to His disciples, "The harvest truly is plentiful, but the laborers are few. Therefore pray the Lord of the harvest to send out laborers into His harvest." '*
>
> (Matthew 9:37–38)

> *'Put in the sickle, for the harvest is ripe.'*   (Joel 3:13)

Are we going to yield to the call and stand in the gap – being obedient and fervent in prayer? (see Ezekiel 22). Do we want our lives to make a difference for eternity? Again, the three questions the Holy Spirit asked me concerning our rewards were:

- 'Did you pay the price?'
- 'Is Spirit-life breathed into it?'
- 'Did you yield to your own initiative?'

What does heaven hold in store for us?

Peter spoke of an inheritance that is incorruptible, undefiled, and that does not fade away, reserved in heaven for us (see 1 Peter 1:4).

No one in heaven will be 'punished', but many in heaven will come to realize they did not become what they could have become, had they allowed the grace of God to work in and through their lives more completely. Their regret will not be eternal, even though their position will be eternally fixed. Heaven would not be heaven if we suffered eternal regret over our loss. Even the least there will be full of joy, his tears of regret wiped away by a loving Shepherd who will lead him to living waters (see Revelation 7:17).

This present life is the most 'heaven' a sinner will ever know and the most 'hell' a Christian will ever experience. This life is only a few years; heaven and hell have no end. There will be no pain in heaven, no joy in hell. There will be no remorse in heaven, no satisfaction in hell; no memory of former things in heaven, no lapse of memory in hell; no torment in heaven, no comfort in hell; no sin in heaven, no righteousness in hell; no devil in heaven, no God in hell; no darkness in heaven, no light in hell; no filthiness in heaven, no holiness in hell.

The Bible teaches that every single person who has ever lived will be in one place or the other, and that once a person has arrived at either place, his or her eternal abode is sealed – without danger, or hope, of that abode ever changing (see Hebrews 9:27).

If you have never been born again, pray this prayer

'Heavenly Father, I call upon You to forgive me of all my sin. I believe that Jesus Christ is Your Son and that His blood was shed for me that I might have forgiveness. So I ask of You right now, that my sins be forgiven and that Jesus Christ come into my life and live through me.

Give me the grace to walk before You, and to depend upon You. I ask that my life reach its full potential and that You will use me to bring increase to Your Kingdom. In the Name of Jesus I ask and believe. Amen.'

For additional copies of this book or other books and tapes by Marilyn or Steve Sampson please write and request a catalogue.

Write to:

Steve Sampson
PO Box 36324
Birmingham, Alabama 35236
USA

Other books available:

By Marilyn Sampson

Never Underestimate the Power of Prayer

By Steve Sampson

Those Who Expect Nothing are Never Disappointed

I Was Always on My Mind

You Can Hear the Voice of God

Breaking the Bondage Barrier – Taking the Limits Off God

You Can't Use Me Today, Lord ... I Don't Feel Spiritual

Enjoying God and Other Rare Events

Don't Talk to Me Now, Lord ... I'm Trying to Pray

Medicine for the Mind (pamphlet)

If you have enjoyed this book and would like to help us to send a copy of it and many other titles to needy pastors in the **Third World**, please write for further information or send your gift to:

Sovereign World Trust
PO Box 777, Tonbridge
Kent TN11 0ZS
United Kingdom

or to the **'Sovereign World'** distributor in your country.

Visit our website at **www.sovereign-world.org**
for a full range of Sovereign World books.